W9-BMR-352
David & Becky Warren

BOB BENSON

Other books by the author

Laughter In The Walls
Come Share The Being
Something's Going On Here

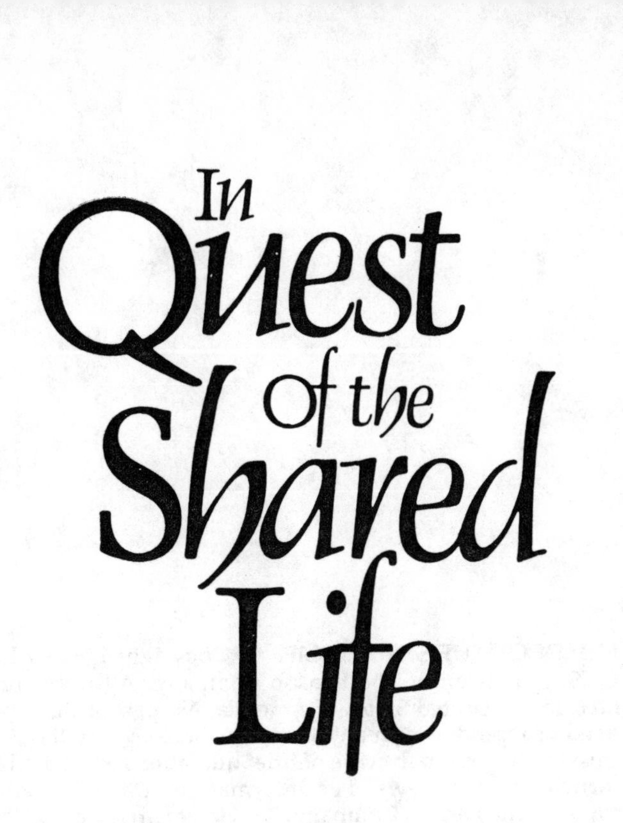

BOB BENSON

IN QUEST OF THE SHARED LIFE © Copyright 1981 by IMPACT BOOKS, a division of The Benson Company. All rights reserved. Printed in the United States of America. No part of this book may be used or reproduced in any manner whatsoever without written permission, except in the case of brief quotations embodied in critical articles and reviews. For information: IMPACT BOOKS, a division of The Benson Company, 365 Great Circle Road, Nashville, Tennessee 37228.

First Printing October 1981

Library of Congress Cataloging in Publication Data
Benson, Bob.
In quest of the shared life.
1. Christian Life—Nazarene Authors. 2. Benson, Bob. I. Title.
BV4501.2B3934 248.4 81-13212
ISBN 0-86608-010-4 AACR2
ISBN 0-914850-55-5 (PBK.)

Library of Congress Catalog Card Number: 81-437-9200

Distributed by The Zondervan Corporation

to Peg—
an old-fashioned girl
who said old-fashioned words with me—
to love and to cherish
and who has done so with style—
for better, for worse,
for richer and for poorer
in sickness and in health
for three decades
of our quest

The author and publisher express appreciation for use of the following copyrighted materials:

At a Journal Workshop, Ira Progoff. Used by permission of Dialogue House Library.

Excerpt from **The Secret of Staying in Love**, by John Powell, S.J., © 1974, Argus Communications. Reprinted by permission.

Jesus, Malcolm Muggeridge. Copyright © 1976 by Harper and Row, Publishers, Inc. Used by permission.

Dorothee Soelle, **Death By Bread Alone**, p. 31. Copyright 1978 by Fortress Press. Used by permission.

M. Scott Peck, **The Road Less Traveled**. Copyright © 1978, Simon and Schuster. Used by permission.

From "When I Say Jesus" by Phil Johnson. © 1973 by Dimension Music. All rights controlled by The Benson Company, Inc. Used by permission.

S. D. Gordon, **Quiet Talks on Prayer**. Copyright © 1980 by Fleming H. Revell Co. Used by permission.

The Inward Journey, Howard Thurman. Used by permission of Friends United Press.

Journey Inward, Journey Outward, Elizabeth O'Connor. Copyright © 1968 by Harper and Row, Publishers, Inc. Used by permission.

From **Noel, Jesus Is Born**, narration by Bob Benson. © Copyright 1979 by Lanny Wolfe Music. All rights reserved. Used by permission.

New Seeds of Contemplation, Thomas Merton. Copyright © 1961 by the Abbey of Gethsemani, Inc. Reprinted by permission of New Directions Publishing Corporation.

Caring, Touching, Feeling, Sidney B. Simon. Copyright © 1976 by Sidney B. Simon. Used by permission of Argus Communications.

Carl R. Rogers, **A Way of Being**, pp. 10 and 22. Copyright 1961 by Houghton Mifflin Company. Reprinted by permission.

Quoted from J. D. Batten, **Tough-Minded Management**, Revised Edition (New York: AMACOM, a division of American Management Associations, 1978), p. 133.

Frederick Buechner, **Wishful Thinking**. Copyright © 1973 by Harper and Row, Publishers, Inc. Reprinted by permission.

Richard J. Foster, **Celebration of Discipline**. Copyright © 1978 by Harper and Row, Publishers, Inc. Reprinted by permission.

Specified excerpts from pp. 125, 126, 127 in "Good-bye to 48th Street" in **The Points of My Compass** by E. B. White. Copyright © 1957 by E. B. White. Reprinted by permission of Harper and Row, Publishers, Inc.

Letters and Papers from Prison, Revised Enlarged Edn.—Dietrich Bonhoeffer (Copyright © 1953, 1967, 1971 by SCM Press Ltd.)

The Crucified God, Jürgen Moltmann. Copyright © 1974 by Harper and Row, Publishers, Inc. Reprinted by permission.

Rainer Maria Rilke, **Letters To A Young Poet**. Translated by M. D. Herter Norton Used by permission of W. W. Norton and Co., Inc.

Robert A. Raines, **To Kiss The Joy**, p. 84. Copyright 1973 by Word, Inc. Used by permission.

Frost, Robert, **A Tribute to the Source.** Copyright © 1979 by David Bradley. Used by permission of Holt, Rinehart and Winston.

Some Scripture quotations, taken from the Books of Genesis and Revelation and from the Gospels of Matthew, Mark, and John, have been paraphrased by the author.

Other Scripture quotations are:

From **The New English Bible**. Copyright © The Delegates of the Oxford University Press and the Syndics of the Cambridge University, 1961, 1970. Reprinted by permission. Quoted verses are indicated by the abbreviation NEB in parentheses.

Contents

Some Words from John 15 As They Speak To Me

I am the Real Vine,
My Father is the Gardener.
He cuts away the barren branches
And the fruitful ones He cleans.
You have already been cleansed
By the words I have spoken to you.
Live in Me as I live in you.
Only as a branch lives in the vine
Can it bear fruit and
Only as you live in Me can you bear fruit.
My Father is the Gardener,
I am the Vine,
And you are the branches.

If you live in Me as I live in you
You will bear much fruit.
Without Me, you cannot do anything.
But if you live in Me
And if My words live in you
You can ask what you will
And it will be yours.
For this is my Father's glory
That you should bear fruit
And so be My disciples.

As the Father has loved Me
I have loved you.
Live in My love
As I have lived in His love.
I have spoken to you so
That I may have joy in you
And so your joy may be complete.

Love each other as I have loved you.
There is no greater love than this,
A man should lay down his life for his friend,
And you are My friends.
I do not call you servants any more,
A servant does not know what his master is doing.
I call you friends
Because I have told you everything,
Everything that my father told me.
You did not choose me, I chose you.
I chose you so that you could go on and bear fruit.
I chose you so that my Father
Could give you all you ask in My name.
This is my commandment to you
Love each other.

Bob Benson, Sr.
1981

Reader's Outline
(John 15)

Introduction

I was in the sixth grade when I began my first serious writing project. It was a novel set in Canada, and it was as colorful as a red Mountie uniform against the driven snow. My friend, Jimmy Bateman, was my editor-typist.

Jimmy was a seventh grader, but he was old for his age. He was the only kid I knew who had his own typewriter. His hideout was a cabin across the road from his house. The cabin was a half-mile or so away if you went around Brush Hill and down Cedarwood. But I could be there in a couple of minutes by crossing the creek behind our house and following the path through the woods.

In writing my novel I made a concerted effort toward genuine authenticity. I took the names of the characters for my story straight from the Canadian map in the geography book. It was the name of the hero which first became a problem. Jimmy laughed so heartily when he saw it that the book died—just as it was beginning to pick up momentum on page four.

I still think "Rupert St. John" is not such a bad name for a Canadian hero. But Jimmy succeeded in driving a promising young writer from the profession. So I was well into my thirties before I really discovered the joy and reward of committing one's thoughts and conclusions to paper.

My interest in putting things in writing was a gift to me from both my parents. I have kept the letters my mother wrote to us when we were away—first in school, and then later in the pastorate. They were usually typed in triplicate. One copy would go to my sister, Laura, who lived in Ohio; another copy to Cally, my sister in college in Kentucky; and the third, to Peg and me.

Each of us has claimed that someone else always got the original and we got a carbon. But carbon or not, these letters were a breath of home. Mom's humor, wisdom, and love were captured in her easy, free-flowing style. The words seemed to have tumbled from her typewriter and from her heart.

Pop, my father, on the other hand, is a serious "working" writer. He edits and reedits and reedits some more. He condenses and lengthens, though usually it is the latter. The process continues until he is satisfied that his words and sentences adequately convey his thoughts and thoroughly describe all the details.

Pop is the historian of the family. Each member of the family has been given a "Benson Book." The 10" x 16" leatherette volume is bound so that it can be added to regularly. It contains articles, family charts, and a history of the Benson bunch dating as far back as 1796 when they crossed the mountains from North Carolina to Tennessee.

But the "Benson Book" is far more than a record of the past. It is also a commentary on our present. Pop is a chronicler of our trips and celebrations. He spends hours carefully recording these events and sending along new pages for our books.

This Christmas, his present to each of the members of the Bob Benson family was a twenty-six-page booklet which he had lovingly put together. The booklet, complete with full-color pictures and running commentary, is entitled, "Bob Benson European Tour—July 22–August 13, 1978." It is a wonderful recollection of a once-in-a-lifetime trip.

If you know my father, you feel as if you are visiting with him when you read:

> Speeding planes, bouncing boxes, taxicabs, airplanes, boats carried us safely from place to place. At times we were relaxed—*hitching a snatch of sleep*. But often we were afoot, moving about, looking, and craning our necks to see the sights of cities, villages, canals, mountains, and lakes.

My mother describes the beginnings of the trip in her more breezy style:

> In the early spring John came home one evening in his usual blithe and exuberant mood, plunked down in his lazy chair, took up *The Banner* and turned to the sports page.
>
> Finally I heard a mumble.
>
> "The Bob Bensons are going to Europe this summer."
>
> "Oh, how nice, how lovely for them," I opined.
>
> "They asked us to go with them."
>
> "Well, wasn't that sweet of them—not that many young people would ask two old grandparents to go along."
>
> Long pause.
>
> "You wouldn't consider going, I'm sure."
>
> Longer pause.
>
> "Well, I just might."
>
> "No. You're kidding."
>
> "Well, we will see."
>
> Back to the sports page.
>
> From that moment on he never had a chance. I started planning to go.

So I do have a legacy as a writer. I only wish I could combine my mother's style and my father's discipline.

My adventures as a "published" writer began inconspicuously enough. My friend, Walt Moore, editor of our local church paper, asked me to do some writing for *The Nazarene Weekly*. His column, "Around the Corner," is so consistently good from week to week that I really didn't want to be in print alongside it. Finally, I did begin to do some little free verse essays about my life and my family. He ran them under the heading, "Lines To Live By." *The Weekly* was the first place I saw anything of my own in print. And it awakened the long-dormant desire of a would-have-been novelist.

I submitted a few of my early essays to a publisher or two and received encouragement from some and rejection slips from others. One editor sent me two rejection slips at once. He enclosed a note advising me that one was for the present manuscript and the other was for my next effort. But, eventually, these essays grew into a book and were published under the title *Laughter In The Walls*.

My second book, *Come Share The Being*, grew out of my studies for the college class at the church and our discussions on Sunday mornings. We were wondering together just what all might be meant by the phrase, ". . . he has given us his promises, great beyond all price, and through them you may . . . come to share in the very being of God" (2 Peter 1:4 NEB). Peg gave the book its title.

During this time I began to travel and speak some on weekends at retreats and conferences and I gathered the thoughts of another year or two around the phrase in Colossians, "The secret is this: Christ in you . . ." (Col. 1:27 NEB). In time they, too, became a book which I called *Something's Going On Here*.

Thus I became the author of three books. To my delight, I discovered that I had engendered a loyal, though small, group of readers. From time to time some of these devoted folks, along with my mother, even began to inquire as to when I was going to write a new book.

In one way I have been ready to write another book

for quite some time. I make it a habit to jot down words, phrases, and thoughts—things I have heard or read or which come to me from time to time. Sometimes I scribble them down in church and sometimes while I'm traveling and almost anywhere in-between. I'm not always prepared for this spontaneous note-taking and so I use whatever is at hand—ticket envelope, calling card (mine or yours), laundry claim stub, boarding pass, or paper napkin.

I stuff this assortment of memos and notes in my coat pockets. At the end of the day, or at least before sending the suit to the cleaners, I will lay them on top of the counter in the bathroom. When Peg cleans she puts my "research" into the top right-hand drawer, which she has reserved for this very purpose.

When the drawer is full, she will transfer the contents to a storage file that looks remarkably like a grocery bag. When I have accumulated about three bags full, I begin to think that it is time to write again. I have had three bags full for a long time. My "research" was complete for another book—stories, poems, incidents, phrases in abundance.

Truthfully, though, the first three books were mostly the same book. The titles were not the same, the covers were changed for obvious reasons, and the stories were different. The reader would meet some new characters, but would faintly remember the plot.

I could write that book again. But somehow I didn't want to write *another* "new" book. I wanted to write a *new* "new" book.

I had come to the place where I wanted a new song to sing, a new story to write, a new verse to quote, a new awareness to share. I wanted a new insight around which to cluster my stories and homilies. I wanted fresh perceptions which would become truth to me.

I don't think I was really searching for some stunning array of facts or a system of belief that would cause everyone to say, "Wow! Think of that!" But I did want some clear and spontaneous understanding that would evoke a quiet "Yes, yes, it is that way for me" from those who read my words.

Discovering something "new" is not as easy as it sounds. Willa Cather once observed, "There are only two or three human stories, and they go on repeating themselves as fiercely as if they had never happened before."

In a real sense, this book is the story of a quest for a new way to see, a new way to hear—a new way of life that would reveal fresh things to be and to say.

This still may not be a *new* "new" book—but it is a quest for one.

But I'm President

"If you had more time, Bob, we could be together more."

Well, yes, Lord, we could. But I'm president of the company—a ministry-oriented company. And I have a big family. I travel and speak a lot on weekends for You. The company is growing and needs much attention from me. These are not easy days in which to live, much less make a company grow. I'm having a hard time keeping it all together.

"I know. I'm not trying to crowd you. And I'm not trying to add to your burdens. I do not want to make it harder for you. I was just reminding you that if you had more time, we could be together more."

For as long as I can remember I have sought the good and the sunshine in life's moments and have found the enjoyment which they brought. Even though I cannot always explain or reflect the depth of my feelings, they are there.

Recently, the kids and I took Peggy out for dinner

to celebrate Mother's Day. We were all dressed up. The boys, Tom and Patrick, and I were in coats and ties; the girls, Leigh and her mother, in lovely summer dresses. It was a fine restaurant with linen and silver and china and crystal and fresh flowers on the tables. The courses were served and, in-between, we had time to laugh and talk and listen to the background music being played softly on the piano. It was a lovely evening for me and I used a phrase to describe my feelings for them: "I'm keyed," meaning only to say how proud I was of all of them and how much it meant to me to be with them. But the words, *I'm keyed,* are words the boys use when they are talking about winning ball games or band contests, connoting excitement and laughter. And when they looked at me sitting at the head of the table quietly and with as much dignity as I could muster, they all burst into laughter. In the candlelight they could not see the tears in my eyes. I did not seem to be able to *look* keyed—but I *was* keyed that night.

Thus, a part of my appreciation for the good which moments bring has come from awareness and recognition. But it has also come from a corresponding sadness which arises from their passing. When something that can never quite be reenacted—even as ordinary an event as a Mother's Day meal—comes to an end, (and all moments are that way) I feel a pensiveness within. This pensiveness gives my life a quality that might be best described as bittersweet. And those moments take on double meaning and richness—because they are—and because they will not always be.

I can remember these mixed feelings from very early in my life. My dad was always a trip-planner and there were vacations in the summers—to Carolina, to Florida, and once as far as Yellowstone National Park. But none of them hold the place in my memory of the fifty-or-so-mile trips down to Ruskin Cave. For several summers, we went there to a combination church retreat and camp meeting for the last ten days of August. My dad was its founder and guiding spirit.

The old hotel, itself an ancient repository of memories, was dilapidated and without furniture or indoor plumbing. Stoves and refrigerators and beds and about everything else had to be hauled down there for the camp. It must have been a tremendous amount of trouble for Dad, and for Mom as well, who was chief cook and bottlewasher. But it wasn't any trouble for me! I have no happier boyhood memories than those of Ruskin. Drinking at the fountain, bathing in the creek, playing volleyball, listening to Brother Raymond Browning's stories, falling in love, singing in the choir, and kneeling in the straw around the altar—all flood my mind with joyful recollection.

But I also remember the last Monday mornings, usually falling on Labor Day. Our family and a few others stayed to help pack up the gear for another year. I would walk across the now-silent grounds, past the empty sidewalks and ballfields. No screams of delight and shock were heard from divers plunging into the cold, clear swimming hole. Chairs were folded and the straw was swept up. The cave auditorium yawned still and quiet. Even then, in my early teens, I somehow knew that moments come—and then they go—and one is left rejoicing and wondering. Rejoicing in what had been —and wondering if he had heard all the music there was to hear and should he have joined in the singing.

But moments are not so important to young men, for they also hear voices that tell them there is always time. They are told, and they tell themselves, that anything which they miss now can be seen or enjoyed later when it comes again. I don't have to tell you when I was born because only *older* men know and write: *Moments come and moments go but they are never repeated.*

And so it was to this part of me His words, "If you had more time we could be together more," began coming and calling to what might be. But it was not only His voice I heard. The call came not from one, but from *all* of the places of my life.

The very *busyness* of the present was gently reminding me of this. By all odds my life was like that of any other business person caught in a struggle to reach the top and to remain there, or to acknowledge and accept the fact that he'll never be there. Though we have the youth and strength to accomplish many things, we do not have the time. A business is a jealous mistress, demanding every waking hour. And even if at last she does decide to let you go home, it is with a briefcase jammed with papers and a mind overflowing with concerns.

We live in a day when activity is respected as well as rewarded. It is an axiom that one never gets very far and certainly not *ahead* on forty hours a week. And the better one can learn to manage well his hours or days, the more likely he is to be given corresponding reward and importance and authority. Thus, time management has become a science in itself.

At the company I had four senior vice-presidents who reported directly to me. They were all younger men, and I felt it my responsibility to inspire and motivate and train them. Together, we were very conscious of how we might improve the use of our time. We knew that, if our planning went well, we would be busier than ever in our successes. We shared with each other anything we read or saw which would help us pack more into the day.

We played little games among ourselves—like seeing how long one could stay at the office and still get across town in time to catch a plane. The time that elapsed between the moment you took a seat on the plane and buckled your seatbelt, and the moment they shut the door and started to push away from the gate was the score. Once, on a one-day trip to Atlanta, a couple of us had a total waiting time of about three minutes—not a record, but a good average. We had all seen the TV commercials showing O. J. Simpson running through airports and jumping over luggage. That day we jumped over O.J. *and* the luggage.

About the only rules to the time games we played were these: you must keep running and you must refill any time you saved.

One of the timesavers we learned was how to get off the phone when you were tired of the conversation in which you had become entangled. The trick was to hang up while *you* were talking. If you put the receiver on the hook when *they* were talking, they would say, "He hung up on me." But if you hung up while you were talking, they never suspected a thing. And by the time they could get back through the switchboard and your secretary, you were unavailable. And my secretary was very good at protecting me.

She kept people who had appointments with me moving smoothly through my office. She would usher them in and close the door. After fifteen minutes or so, she would call me on the phone to ask if I was having a good time. If I answered yes, the visitor was given more time. If I told her no, it was only a moment or so before she came in to remind me, as well as the visitor, that I had another appointment in a few minutes.

In the days when the company was all in one room and Dad was the president, he had an unwritten rule. When he began to drum his fingers discreetly on the desk, somebody was to go next door and call him on the phone. He had spent all the time he wished to spend with that person. Drumming his fingers was his *rescue me* signal.

We all have used our timesaver devices to add new activities to our schedules, so that we are actually busier than we were before we saved the time.

When my dad was traveling for a living, he used to go up to Washington, D.C., and then over into Pennsylvania. He would catch the Tennessee Central night train and sleep into Knoxville. Then he would change to the Southern and ride into Washington. He had had a restful night and most of the day to prepare himself for the calls he was going to make.

Now we go by plane so we can work all day and into the evening to get our desks in some sort of shape to leave before rushing to the airport to catch the 9:05. We get to bed at the hotel late and are up early to begin the day and finally come home on the redeye at midnight. We don't see our kids that night because they are already in bed. And we don't see them the next morning either because we have to get to the office early to make up for being away the day before.

Practically, flying to Washington saves nearly a full day of travel time. Realistically, the time saved only gets filled up again with more than can be accomplished.

I sometimes think that at least part of what Jesus said about a businessman's having a harder time getting to heaven than a camel's going through the eye of a needle had to do with the fact that there just is not any time open in the appointment book. If the gate was wide enough to drive a Mack truck through, it would still be next month before it could even be considered.

And I do not think that it is much easier for a mother to get the kids on the school bus in the morning; pick them up in the afternoon; take one to ball practice, one to the dentist, and one to cheerleading class; and still have everyone home for dinner in time to get to the PTA meeting only to learn that Mary has volunteered her to be room mother.

The *busyness* of the present was also saying to me, "If you had more time. . . ." there are walks to take, people to know, poems to write, things to be, and truths to learn, "if you had more time. . ."

The *stepping stones* of the past were also echoing this truth to me. I am borrowing the word *stepping stones* from Ira Progoff. In his book, *At A Journal Workshop*, he defines them as:

> . . . the significant points of movement along the road of an individual's life. They stand forth as indicators of the inner connectedness of each person's existence, a continuity of development that maintains itself despite the vicissitudes and the apparent shifting of directions that occur in the course of life.

The stepping stones that lead through the jumbled maze of my life—the people I have met, the things that have happened to me, the events that have occurred around me, and the roads that I have both taken and not taken—all lead in the same direction. And these rites of passage or rituals of transformation are becoming more readily visible to me.

There was a time when I could not see some of them for the tears. Sometimes I was so filled with impatience and frustration I refused even to look. It seemed to me that more than one thing was leading me away from the pathway which I thought I had been chosen to follow. It was easy for me to use such labels as *interruption, detour, setback, tragedy, misfortune,* and *unfair*. But when I look back now at the pathway which brought me here, everything seems to have served a common purpose. And in its way—whether by resistence or by aid and comfort—it has led me to this present place. And while there are places to which I would not choose to return, there isn't anywhere I wish I had not gone. For each of them brought something to me which has become a part of what I bring to today.

Indeed, it is true that the deepest and most precious truths that are mine to enjoy and express have often come to me on the wings of things I did not choose. One of the deepest lessons we learned as a family came tagging along with a very serious illness.

And that illness just came upon us. A routine test brought the word *cancer* into the vocabulary of our immediate family. With it came all the fear and uncertainty that word has the power to evoke. But it also brought a genesis of closeness which we had not known before. It turned our focus to the deepest values in life and in each other.

I began this book in our old house by the lake and as I was writing these lines, Tom and Patrick were coming down the driveway from school. I raised the window to wave to them from my study over the carport. They shouted back to me and started across to the house. Leigh had just come in from college for the weekend and she ran out of the house to meet them. As I watched from above, they ran into each other's arms under the basketball goal. It was a lovely scene for a father to remember. Our acquaintance with the specter of separation brought new meanings to our reunions.

Sheldon Vanauken has made the C. S. Lewis term, *severe mercy,* familiar to us all with his book by the same title. These severe mercies are usually unvolunteered for. They usually thrust themselves upon us and we are forced to wrestle with them for their meaning. And when the dawn comes, we, like Jacob, will be limping a little but we will have been given new names. It is often these things which bring us to sudden stops and give us pause to reevaluate meanings and reconsider values that have been there for us all the time.

It is true that uncertainties seem intolerable at the time. But it is here we begin to see that "Even the life of faith is, in practice, full of contingencies and rightly so. That is why it is a life of faith." It is here that we begin to learn to trust the processes or as Robert Raines says, "to give God some elbow room."

And this inner realization that there was a thread that bound my life into a whole was also saying to me, "If you had more time. . ." This increasing certainty that my life is headed somewhere was calling me into the presence of the One who both knows and controls its direction.

There is one other significant place from which the voice was speaking to me in addition to the *busyness of the present* and the *stepping stones of the past.* It came to me out of a pattern of study that has been mine.

I once heard a missionary tell a very moving story about an African man to whom he had given a copy of the Bible. The African was so grateful for the gift and so profuse in his thanks that the missionary was puzzled a few months later when they met. For the Bible was battered and torn and it looked as if many of the pages were missing. "I thought you would have taken better care of the Bible I gave you," he remarked. "I assumed you wanted it and would treasure it." And the African man replied, "It is the finest gift I ever received. It is such a wonderful book that I gave a page to my father and a page to my mother, and then I gave a page to everyone in the village."

I certainly believe in the programs which encourage and aid us to read the Bible through in a year. My only misgivings surface during my usual founderings in the doldrums of Deuteronomy in mid-March. But I also believe there is great value in centering oneself in a given place in the Word and lingering there until it has had time to make an indelible impression on one's life.

It probably would do us all good—we who have so many Bibles in so many translations—to have only a page for a while—until we had learned it, until we had loved it, until it was ours in truth.

I read about a book entitled *The Joys of Super Slow Reading*. In the book there is an account of a man who was imprisoned during World War II. He was only able to take a single book with him when he was captured. Since he did not know how long it was going to be before he was rescued, he determined he would make that one book last. And he rationed out its words and pages to himself.

It might be a good exercise for each of us to take some small portion of Scripture and, instead of approaching it with the idea of finishing it quickly, we might try to see how long we could make it last.

About three years ago I began to read the first seventeen verses of the fifteenth chapter of John's gospel. Although at the time, it was not my intent to dwell there for an indefinite period, it has worked out that way. I did not know how long I would be reading the verses or how long they would be speaking to me. But they are words of tremendous import and I am still learning from them. Jesus, in this place, is describing the relationship of the *shared life*. He uses such words and phrases as:

dwell, abide, live
choose, ordain, appoint
prune, cleanse, cut away
nothing, everything
servants, friends
joy, love, death
fruit, much fruit
fruit that shall last
gardener, vine, branches.

His descriptions and invitations to a life lived in Him and in His love and under the Father's protection reminded me again and again that the moments when this should be true for me were slipping by and could never be recovered. And they have joined with the circumstances of my life, both past and present, in saying, "If you had more time, we could be together more."

The things that follow in the book are those things that have come to me as I have attempted to begin to bring the workings of my life into the relationship he describes in John 15.

Gradually it came to be decision time.

Leigh said it for me.

She hadn't been sixteen very long when she announced to the family that she was *going steady*. Well, she told her mother and the rest of us found out. She had been dating this guy for a little while, but now it was *official*. She had the class ring with all the tape to prove it.

What a fine romance!

Leigh was happy because she had a boyfriend. Peg was happy because he was a courteous, fine-looking boy with good manners, who spent part of each visit to our house showering his attention on Leigh's mother.

And I was happy . . . happy because he lived fifty miles away and could only come to see Leigh once a week. Phone calls were long distance, so even they were few and short. What a fine romance. It was all a dad could hope for his only daughter, if she insisted on having a boyfriend.

She was happy. He was happy. Peg was happy and I was happy. Everybody was happy. Everybody except one football player who had been in school with Leigh since they were in fifth grade. He had been there the first day she had worn her braces to school. He had been there many, many months later when they were gone and she had a set of lovely, straight teeth behind her smile.

He had been there the first morning she had worn her glasses and also the day she had put them aside for contacts. He had watched as her mother finally gave up on the short, easy-to-fix hairdo and as Leigh's face was framed by long tresses that spilled over her shoulders.

For some reason, *he* was not happy.

"What a waste, Leigh. You are just too young to go steady," said the football player. "It's all right to date that old boy once a week, but there are six other nights. To sit home all week. What a waste! You are just too young to go steady."

Sooner or later Leigh and the tall, dark, and largely absent boyfriend did decide to stop going steady and be "just friends." As soon as the football player heard this news, he asked her for a date. On the first date he asked her to go out the next night. On the second night he said to her,

"Will you go steady with me?"

"No," she replied.

"Be *my* steady girlfriend," he urged.

"I can't be yours. I just got myself back."

Leave it to your children to put big, complicated things into short, simple words. What I had to do was to "get myself back." So this is a book about one man's effort

to regroup,
to slow down,
to simplify,
to free up,
to gather himself together again
so that he might learn
new and deeper ways in Him.

In the Scene

Ignatius of Loyola, in his book *Spiritual Exercise,* encourages one to relive the events of Scripture by entering into them as if living part of the drama. He instructs his students to make themselves present in the gospel by using all of their physical senses. With imagination, one must try to see and hear and feel and smell and taste until he is a part of the event described. Mark Link, in an interesting little book called *You,* terms this the process of putting oneself *in the scene*.

For instance, try to imagine yourself trying to keep up with a crowd of people who are following Jesus. He is just coming up from the shore and He is walking with Jairus, the president of the synagogue. For twelve years now you have had a blood disease. Periodic hemorrhaging has left you so weak that you can barely keep up with the crowd.

You have spent all your money going to doctors in your own village as well as those nearby, but you really aren't much better. As a matter of fact, you are weaker and thinner this afternoon than you have ever been. You have heard a little about this Jesus and how He has healed some people.

Walking along, you are impressed with the notion that if you could just touch His robe, you would get better. Before the part of you that is skeptical can overcome the impulse, you have pushed your way between the couple in front of you. You reach out and touch Him.

Can you feel the coarse, woolen cloth of His robe? It is still damp, for He has just come out of the boat. Can you smell the dust as it rises around you, kicked by a hundred scuffling sandals? Do you hear the woman mumbling because you jostled her trying to get closer to Jesus? Do you see Jesus as he turns to you?

Now look into His face and tell Him what you did. Hear Him call you "child." Feel the warmth of His smile as He bids you go. Sense His peace as it pushes the darkness of discouragement and the gloom of disease from you. Can you imagine being suddenly well after all your years of illness? Run toward home with the news—you're well!

As we read the Scripture we need to learn to put ourselves "in the scene." We need to leave our boats as He calls us; we need to eat the bread as He breaks it; we need to see our daughter healed; we need to hear His words. We need to be there.

I have been trying to "live myself" into this Scripture place in the fifteenth chapter of John. It is set in the last days and hours of Christ's life on earth. These are tender, intimate times.

Even the words of Christ seem to take on added depth. He was never an idle talker but each of these words are worthy of study, for they are poignant with the meanings of love and obedience. They have meanings that only come when there is more to be said than there is time to say it.

It was late in his life and late in the day and now late in His last hours with His disciples. Only the most important things of all could be said.

John Powell presents in *The Secret of Staying in Love* a passage entitled: "Entry From A College Girl's Journal." It describes the feelings of someone who is trying to imagine her thoughts if she had to measure her life in terms of hours. The entry reads:

> If I had only a short time to live, I would immediately contact all the people I had ever really loved, and I'd make sure they knew I had really loved them. Then I would play all the records that meant most to me, and I would sing all my favorite songs. And oh! I would dance. I would dance all night.
>
> I would look at my blue skies and feel my warm sunshine. I would tell the moon and the stars how lovely and beautiful they are. I would say "goodbye" to all the little things I own, my clothes, my books, and my "stuff." Then I would thank God for the great gift of life, and die in His arms.

It was that time for Jesus. There were only enough moments for Him to make sure "they knew He had really loved them" and to thank His Father "for the great gift of life."

There were no plans for writing these things down. What was done and what was said would have to be remembered. As long as they were all together, the disciples could help each other recall. But if any one of them moved to the next village, only what he remembered was his. And so Jesus tells them they must eat this meal again and again so they would remember.

We need to be there, too. So we also will always remember. We need to hear, see, feel, smell, and taste:

the faint smell of fear
the quiet groaning of doubt
the water He uses to wash our feet
the towel with which He dries them
the bread that He dipped in the gravy.

And most of all, in the scene of impending disaster, doubt, and denial, we need to hear *the things that He is saying*. And to realize their greater significance because *He is saying them now*—in these last hours.

Maybe He could have said these things at the beginning—but not now. Perhaps when it was the morning of the cause—but now it was night. Only yesterday, it seems, He had started out. He had chosen them and they had left to go with Him. They had been filled with the newness of His call and the brightness of the adventure. To be a part of the unfolding hopes and promises of God to a nation had filled this little band of men with excitement. Their faith had made His heart glad. The crowd had been large and eager. The opposition had not yet decided that someday this matter would have to be finally settled on a cross.

New causes are like that.

The office is an attic and the desk is an orange crate. There isn't any stationery and the "e" on the typewriter sticks, but it doesn't matter because hearts are full. Everything rushes forth in excitement and joy. *Maybe back then—but not now.*

The things Jesus is saying in these closing hours would have seemed more appropriate in some high point when He was alone with them. Perhaps when it was becoming apparent that the truth was finally beginning to take root in their hearts. Or when he could begin to hope the truth would grow to bear fruit in the days ahead when He would no longer be with them.

The words He is saying now could have been said

on a sunny afternoon like that day over near Caesarea Philippi. Jesus and His disciples were seated in the shade of a tree on a peaceful hillside and Jesus was asking them about the reactions of the crowds.

"Who do they say that I am?"

"They don't seem to know. Some of them say you are John the Baptist and some of them say Elijah or Jeremiah. Some think you are one of the other prophets."

He moves a little and turns so that He is looking at them all. Now He brings the question into the tiny, uneven circle of men for an answer.

"And who do *you* say that I am?"

"You are Christ. You are the Son of God," Simon blurts out.

A smile moves across the Master's face. He touches Simon's shoulder. A tear forms and makes its way down across His cheek. His voice is almost overcome with happiness and pride.

"Simon, bless you; you big rascal, bless your heart. You didn't hear that in the crowd. My Father told you that."

Maybe He could have said these things then—but not now. It was hard to believe that three years had sped by. But they had and now the hour had come. The crowds on the hillsides and the noisy courtyards and streets are far away now from this quiet feast of fellowship and betrayal.

What is happening now is a tragic occasion of defeat and failure. Maybe all that had gone before will be for nothing. Maybe His life will be taken for no good purpose at all. And the cause that had almost danced its way across the countryside will probably be scattered into so many pieces that it can never be put together again.

These men—the soil into which He had planted

the seeds of truth. These men—out of whom the gospel was to grow and spread. These men—who were supposed to know the most and believe the deepest. These men—who had dared to step out and go with Him. These men—are about to go back home in failure and dishonor.

Maybe before—but not now. Yet, His words of love and faith and hope for them are spoken loudest and clearest in this time and place where it seems they should not be said at all.

They were in Jerusalem. Six days ago they had come down from Ephraim, a little country village a dozen or so miles to the north. The city itself was crowded with people who had come to purify themselves before the Passover Festival. They looked for Jesus because they wanted to hear Him teach. Maybe, too, there would be another miracle like the raising of Lazarus which had taken place not long ago in nearby Bethany.

The chief priests and elders were also looking for Him. They waited with orders that anyone with information about Him should bring it to them so that they might arrest Him.

Jesus spent those five days before the Feast of the Passover teaching in the Temple in the daytime and withdrawing to the quiet of Olivet's hillside at night to rest and pray.

On the day of the Feast He sends Peter and John ahead to make some preparations. The instructions He gives them are words that will gently test their faith and obedience. He tells them to go into the city and they will see a man carrying a jar of water. They are to follow him and when he enters a house, they are to knock on the door and ask the householder if there is a room where they may eat the Passover supper. And he will have a place for them and they are to make preparations there.

And they did what He told them and it was just like He had said.

In the evening Jesus and His Twelve make their way into the city for the Passover supper. Jesus, knowing that His hour has come, goes to His Last Supper with the disciples. Like the Passover supper itself, with the lamb and the bitter herbs, their meal would later bring back both good memories and bad. The occasion would be recalled with hope and peace as they recounted the things He had told them there. But they would also remember that night with shame. Each of them would not forget his own response to the lovely last things He had said to them all.

Nothing is told of the walk into the city or of entering the room or even of the beginning of the meal. But all during supper, Jesus demonstrates His deep love for them all.

In word and deed He reaches out instinctively to the neediest of the group. Always His heart is the heart of a shepherd and, midway through the meal, He turns to Judas.

Judas had made some preparations for this night also. He had been to the chief priests and the captains of the Temple police and promised to deliver Jesus to them.

It really wasn't the money. The cause already seemed lost. The truth was that he really feared a little for his own safety in this crowded city. And so a secluded place was selected where there would be no danger of riot.

And now Judas sits at the table with Jesus and his fellow followers. He waits for the moment when the bargain will be sealed. Alone in his thoughts, he eats his supper and slips closer and closer to the precipice of no return. A little while now and it will be too late—it will be *done*.

Jesus, knowing that one of the men He loves is about to fall, rises from the table and performs two last deeds of hope and tenderness.

He lays aside his garments and ties a towel around His waist. Taking a basin of water, He begins to wash the feet of each of the twelve men at the table. Water and love splash over the feet of Judas, as if to say it is not too late for these feet to walk the ways to which they have been called.

"You are altogether clean," He tells them when He has finished, "but not every one of you."

Jesus, always kind, always compassionate, still does not point His finger at Judas. Now He seats Himself at the table.

"One of you has turned against Me. One of you is going to betray Me," He tells them in a voice heavy with grief.

"Lord, who is it?"

"It is the man with whom I share bread when I have dipped it into the dish."

And in a custom that was usually reserved for honored guests and for very special friends, Jesus takes bread and soaks it in the dish and offers it to Judas. Judas takes it and, as he eats, the betrayal begun in the Temple is completed.

"Do quickly what you have to do" echoes in Judas' ears as he moves out into the night.

In the silence Jesus looks at the twelve places at the table and at the eleven men. Twelve places—eleven men. He begins again to review with them all that the Father had told Him: why He came, where He came from, and why He will be going away. He speaks to them so there will be no question in their minds about all that has gone before.

In this hour the deepest tenets of their faith are fraught with doubts and questions. One by one they interrupt Him, as if His words are strange and new to their ears and their hearts.

"I will be with you a little longer and then I will be going."

"But where are You going and why can't I go with You?"

"I am going to the Father's house and I will prepare a place for you and I will come back so you will know the way."

"But we do not know where You are going, so how can we know the way?"

"I am the way; I am the truth; and I am the life. I am the only way to the Father."

"Well, show us the Father and then we will not ask You any more questions."

"You have seen Me so you have seen the Father. I am in the Father and the Father is in Me."

"What has happened? Why are You just showing Yourself to us and not to the world?"

These eleven men—soon they will sleep while He prays. They will run while He is arrested. They will hide while He dies. But they are still His men, and in confidence and hope He speaks to them. "You will all scatter and go to your own home and leave me alone. But I will not be by myself because the Father is with me. And I want you to remember what I am telling you now. Remember it when you are home so that you will be at peace. In the world there is trouble, but in me there is peace. Don't be discouraged because victory is mine. I have overcome the world."

Finally, before they leave their sanctuary and go across the Kidron ravine to the place of arrest, Jesus prays for them.

At our house it is a custom to join hands in a circle as we pray. We do this as a family and, when there are other people there, we just make the circle larger. I have been accused of always getting between Peggy and Leigh or any other pretty ladies present and then asking someone to lead us in a long prayer. Pray for everybody and all their relatives and then the missionaries and all theirs, too. Pray a filibuster if you like. And I can just stand there holding hands with those two fair ladies.

I don't know if the disciples were kneeling or if they were standing in a circle with hands joined as Jesus began to pray. But, to me, this must have been one of the great prayer places to be. I am trying to think what His words might have meant to us if we had been there in that hour as He looked up into His Father's face and prayed. Just like the others, we are filled with fear and doubt. We wish it were not so when He tells us that we will run for home and leave Him all alone. Still we know that we are probably going to do just that. Listen to Him as He prays for us.

Sometimes we are prayed *over*. Sometimes we are prayed *about*. And sometimes we are prayed *at*. But this time we are going to be prayed *for*—by the One who knows us and rejoices in us and cares openly for us. He will remind the Father of all that we have done. And He asks the Father to help us in all that we are going to do.

The words that He prays are overflowing with His adoration and thanks. There is such deep warmth revealed, both in the words of the *prayer* and in the heart of the *pray-er,* that it can only be described as exultation. There is His heartfelt pride and joy as He thanks His Father for the very gift of us.

We often speak of Jesus as being God's unspeakable Gift to us. And it is easy to understand why Paul would give us this phrase to use about Him. But here He is talking to the Father about *us,* and the word He uses is *gift.* And that is hard to comprehend. For Jesus to bother with us at all is amazing enough. To think He gave His life when, at the very best, He would get only *us*. It can only be explained or understood when we think of Him as "obedient unto death." But in this prayer His word is not duty or task or responsibility. His word is *gift*. Not only is He going to the cross, but He is rejoicing over us as He does.

We need to transport ourselves back across history into a room where Jesus is praying over eleven men and twelve chairs. Because we need to hear Him say that we are His glory, we are His gift from the Father.

During a recent Christmas season our evening paper, *The Nashville Banner*, carried a beautiful little story related by Red O'Donnell. In his column, Red gathers up the city in a record of quotes, birthdays, and stories overheard on the 5:00 A.M. Madison bus. One little girl was reported as suggesting to her mother that she was glad there was no room in the inn. Of course, her mother wanted to know why. The answer was:

"Because it makes a better story."

And I am glad there was this Last Supper. Because it is a story in which we can find ourselves.

If it had been a tale like King Arthur and his Knights of the Round Table, it would be hard to imagine ourselves included. I don't have a horse or a suit of armor. And even if I did, I don't like to ride. But I even like riding better than fighting.

This is the Last Supper. It is not a gathering of the skilled or the courageous. It is not an evening planned for the top salesmen or the honor students or the medal-winners. Rather, it is a last meal shared by Jesus and His band of ordinary men. It is one more time to tell them of His love for them in spite of everything—their jealousies, misunderstandings, failures, and disbelief. Indeed, *because* of all these things, He has planned this last meal together.

And we *belong* at this table. Each of us bring credentials of weakness, fear, and failure. We are a part of this group.

We *need to be* at this table, for we need to feel His love meeting us at the deepest places of our lives. And to realize that it is being spoken out of the deepest place of His.

We need to be "in the scene."

It's You! It's You!

Jesus came to be experienced.

I know it isn't to my credit, but I have never really desired to go to the Holy Land. Perhaps I have seen too many slides taken by those who have.

One of the conventions Peg and I attended as a part of my business was the Church Music Publishers' Association. The gathering was always rather informal, and the evening programs sort of evolved through the volunteering of the members in attendance. And people who have been to the Holy Land and have their own slides are usually the "volunteering" type.

One evening we were "visiting" the Holy Land in this manner, and the host was showing us the place where he thought the children of Israel had crossed the Red Sea. It was not the traditional site, but he was sure this was where they had really gone across. He had taken pictures from every conceivable angle—behind trees and under rocks—to illustrate that this was the most likely spot for that great procession of people to have come down to the shore and filed over.

After all his "scientific" research and evidence about the Red Sea crossing, he showed some pictures of a bush which was supposed to be like the "burning bush" Moses had turned aside to see. The photographer frankly admitted that the actual tree probably wasn't like this one, but he had taken a picture because it was what he had always thought it *should* look like. So much for science.

I think some of my reluctance in visiting the Holy Land is rooted in description such as that of Malcolm Muggeridge in his classic book, *Jesus, The Man Who Lives.* He was in the Holy Land for the purpose of producing the commentary for three television programs on the New Testament story. One day they were filming in the hills outside Bethlehem.

> Sure enough, in the fields there was a shepherd with his flock—sheep and goats duly separated, just as required. When he caught sight of us and our equipment he picked up one of his sheep in his arms. Then, when he had established his posture, and our cameraman was focusing for a shot, he put down the sheep and came forward to haggle over his fee. It was after settling this unseemly transaction, and getting our footage of the shepherd and his flock, that we went into the Church of the Nativity, having the greatest difficulty in making our way because of the press of beggars and children offering picture postcards, rosaries, and other souvenirs for sale . . . The Holy Land, as it seemed to me, had been turned into a sort of Jesusland, on the lines of Disneyland.

I am finally thinking of going to the Holy Land, though, with my son Mike. He is attending the seminary from which I graduated. When he finishes, he will have a higher degree than I received and that

doesn't seem quite fair to me. I can complete some Bible study in the Holy Land and be awarded the same degree he is receiving. Also it will be nice to walk in the same commencement procession with Mike. Besides, I do not want my kids more educated than I am if I can help it.

I think, too, I am ready to see and feel the countryside that Jesus saw and felt. I would like to feel what Muggeridge described as "the transformation of a tourist attraction into an authentic shrine."

For He came into history at this particular place, and from then until now His followers have revered it. The land He not only created but walked and crawled and ate and slept and lived and died on is a "holy land." But the significance of His coming was not that He came to make that tiny bit of geography forever holy. He came to show us and to tell us that whenever and wherever He breaks into the times and places of life they, too, can become "holy." He came *then* and *there* so that we might know that He can come *here* and *now* to make the land of our life—a holy land.

To walk the roads He walked must be inspirational and life-changing. But our lives can only be lifted and changed as we realize that He is indeed walking the roads we walk. It will not happen as we go to be where He *was*—it will happen as we realize that He *is* where we *are*.

Jesus Christ came to be *experienced*. In her book, *Death by Bread Alone*, Dorothee Soelle tells us: "The language of religion is the vehicle of collective experience and it is meaningful only when it speaks of experience and addresses itself to experience."

John, in his gospel and in his letters, writes about Jesus in terms of experience. He only declares what he has seen and heard.

The Word was made flesh,
the Word lived among us,
we saw His glory
of His fullness we all received,
the life was visible to us,
we heard Him with our ears,
we saw Him with our eyes,
we touched Him with our hands,
we are in Him who is real.

After speaking a time or two up in Idaho, I became acquainted with a young school teacher there. We talked about experiences and about writing. She told me that she sometimes wrote down the things that she felt deeply. And I asked her to send some of her writings along to me.

Later, she wrote me a letter and enclosed some things she had written. She told me it helped to know that someone else was reading them, but she was also glad I was far enough away that she didn't have to see me afterwards.

One lovely little essay on *worth* was included along with some of her other pieces. She concluded her letter about her writings by admitting they were probably not original ideas. "Everything I have written I have probably heard before; either I read it or heard it in a sermon. But hearing words and nodding my head is not the same as *realizing an idea in my own words.*"

Nothing that happens at some other place; nothing that happens at some other time; nothing that happens to someone else will be quite enough for you. He must come to you in the times and places of your life in ways that you can recognize and relate. He must come to you in *your own words.*

I didn't know it at the time, but one of my last official acts as president of The Benson Company was the Christian Booksellers' Association Convention of

1979. Held each summer, the CBA Convention is one of the highlights of a religious publisher's business life. All the new product for the fall is displayed, which means it is the beginning point for the most important selling season of the year. Obviously, much of the winter and spring planning and production is built around getting ready for this important week.

The company also holds its summer sales conference prior to the event, and all of the regional salesmen and their wives are there. From the opening of the sales conference through the final awards banquet, it is both a wearying and an exciting time.

The CBA met in St. Louis that year, and it brought back a host of memories for me. Almost twenty years before, Peg and I had gone for our first time to represent the company at the convention which was held in the Kiel Auditorium in St. Louis. Mary Davis, and her husband Gene, on vacation from Genesco, made up the rest of the staff. The sign over the tiny eight-by-eight booth was homemade and we displayed all of our recordings—both of them—and our songbooks on the one table that was furnished with the booth. Gene handed out key chains with the company name and address. Peg smiled and greeted everyone. She has never seen a stranger! And Mary and I wrote orders for our meager line of religious music. In retrospect, we were not the rage of the convention. The dealers, though, are a wonderful group of people and some of them we met there are still friends today.

Now we had grown into a sixteen-by-fifty-foot booth and it took all fourteen salesmen a full day to uncrate the display unit and "set up the store."

It was a particularly busy week for me. There were people to see, meetings to attend, negotiations for distribution rights of another firm, and other "presidential" duties to perform. I was deep in the throes of personal decisions for the future and so it was a very hard week for me. It was one of those weeks when you are supposed to be smiling the smile that makes everyone else smile. It's part of your job as president. Company morale and *esprit de corps* seem to take their cue from your confidence and optimism—only inside, you really feel like crying. One of *those* weeks—you know the kind.

My son Tom was with me and I talked a lot to him. He was kind enough to listen and it helped because he did. When I didn't have to be somewhere, I spent the time with Tom. We stayed in a hotel across the street from the old courthouse where the Dred Scott decision was made—very close to the St. Louis Arch.

Some irreverent wag has described the Arch as the world's largest McDonald's sign. But it really is a magnificent architectural and engineering accomplishment. We went through the museum underneath the Arch, and read the literature describing the period of history that the Arch represents. I was reading to keep from being nervous while waiting to ride to the top in a contraption shaped much like a barrel. If Tom hadn't been there, I wouldn't have gone. But he was and I did.

The brochure said, *"The thing was done"* on October 28, 1965. The architect who had conceived the design in a competition for the privilege submitted his plans in 1947, but he had passed away before the Arch was completed. "For him *the thing was never done.*" The article concluded:

> The Arch commemorates Thomas Jefferson and the Louisiana Purchase, the process we call Westward Expansion, and the lives of otherwise unknown individuals who settled the West. It recalls our past, suggests our future. It shows our capabilities and our limitations.

> The Arch belongs to a nation, but also belongs to a person: you. Risk a moment. Take a long, slow look at your monument as it soars, welcomes, and entices. Decide for yourself: What does this monument mean to me? And then, and only then, *the thing is done*.

And in a very deep sense the gospel is only *done for you* when you can hear these words of Jesus as personal words: "You are cleansed by the words that I spoke *to you*."

Our lives are filled with words. "When can you send the payment?" "Where is my shirt?" "When will you have this completed?" "Don't you think you need this to protect your family?" "He hit me first!" "Your car has to have a new transmission." "The cost-of-living index rose again this month by 1 percent!" "Your blood pressure is much higher than it should be."

These are the words of our lives. And it is among them that we must hear Him speaking to us.

It was not really any easier for the disciples. In my opinion one of the great short stories of the New Testament is found in the last chapter of Luke. The story begins very early on Easter Sunday at the tomb of Jesus in Jerusalem. It ends some seven miles away in Emmaus.

Mary Magdalene, Joanna, Mary, the mother of James, and some other women took spices they had prepared to the place where Jesus was buried. When they got there, the stone was rolled aside from the entrance. They went inside and found the body gone. They were standing there, utterly at a loss, when two men in bright and shining garments appeared beside them. In the women's terror one of the men reminded them of Jesus' words about His death and resurrection.

Then the group of women began to recall what He had said and went to find the eleven and all the others and tell them what had happened. But nobody would believe them.

Later that day two of the men set out on their way to the village of Emmaus. Of course, they were talking about all that had happened in Jerusalem that week. And Jesus came and walked along with them. But they didn't recognize Him.

It has always interested me that they did not know who He was. More than that, though, it has always intrigued me that He did not tell them. I have wondered why He didn't rush up to them exclaiming, "It's Me? It's Me! It's over! I'm back! We won! It's Me! It's Me!"

The thing I am beginning to see is that it seemed more important for Him to wait until *they* said, "It's You! It's You!"

I think I can imagine a little of what Jesus must have been trying to do. It must be like encouraging your infant son to take his first steps. With open arms you wait.

"Come on, come to Daddy. Let go of Mommy's hand and come to me," you say.

You almost lean over and take his hand and pull him across the space that separates you. But that would not be walking. That would be pulling, wouldn't it? Walking is when he takes a step all by himself.

So I think Jesus is leaning as far as He can and still allowing them to come to Him in faith. He reminds them of the things Moses and all the prophets had written about Him. Surely, now they know. Hint after hint, clue after clue, until there was hardly anything left to say except, "It's Me! It's Me!"

Still, nobody said, "It's You."

The sun had begun to drop in the West when they reached the village, but still they had not uttered the words of recognition. And now their roads must part.

They were going home. He was going on. It was now or never. What should He do? Should He tell them now or should He wait for another time and another place?

I believe that Jesus' heart jumped within Him when one of the men asked Him to stay for supper and the night. Time—more time for them to take the first faltering steps of faith.

It was one of those evenings when father brings home an unexpected guest. The mother straightened the extra bedroom and apologized for the supper. The kids were on their best behavior, having been reminded in the kitchen to mind their manners. They gathered at the table. They asked Jesus to return thanks. They aren't sure who He is but He must be religious because He knows all that Scripture.

He took the bread and said the blessing. And then He broke it and passed it down the table to each of them.

And they said, "It's You!"

And He was gone from them.

I think I know what happened at the supper table that night. I can imagine what made them suddenly know who had walked with them all the way and was now at the table with them.

In a family the size of ours, it is hard to get everybody to the table on time. Somebody's always hollering, "Just a minute," back down the stairs. And it always takes longer than a minute. And then somebody else gets there a little early and helps Peg put the food on the table. They put everything but the broccoli, maybe, where they can reach it from where they sit. They even corral the salt and pepper and the butter. Although it's against the rules, occasionally someone even butters his bread before the rest of us get there. I am reluctant to admit it, but I have had to call on someone to return thanks who had to pray for food of which we were about to partake as well as some that was in the process of being "partaken." It's hard to pray with a hot roll in your mouth.

Finally, though, the minute is up and we are all there. We join hands and say together:

Happy is he whose help and hope
are in the Lord his God,
Who keeps faith forever
and gives food to the hungry.
Praise the Lord.

Amen.

So now I'm down at the daddy's end and the food is somewhere clustered around the one who brought it to the table.

"Please pass the potatoes."
"Please pass the tomatoes."
"Please pass the meat."
"Please pass the salt."

You would think people would pass the pepper, too, when you asked for the salt, wouldn't you?

"Please pass the butter."

And by now you are beginning to get some indication that they really wish you would stop bothering them so they could eat.

You don't have any bread, but by now you decide you'll just put the butter on the potatoes and forget it.

And then somebody, usually Peg, says, "Daddy doesn't have any bread. Someone pass Daddy the bread."

I'm believing that the thing that brought forth the glad recognition was just this. Jesus said, "Cleopas doesn't have any bread. Somebody pass Cleopas the bread."

And Cleopas said, "It's You! It's You!"

We can study and discuss what Jesus came to do for mankind. We can learn all the prophecies about Jesus and give our assent to them. They can even become our creeds and beliefs. But it is when we realize that He knows we do not have any bread, and that He is starting it down the table to us, that we suddenly know who He is. He has been with us in our journey. He has been there all the time. *He is with us.*

Only such times of experience—only such moments can bring validity to religion. If we can hear His voice, we do not need any other proof. And if we cannot, then no other proof will do.

Of course, there are reasons for believing in God. Theologians and thinkers have gathered them up for us and distilled them into a few classical arguments. The order and the purpose of the universe certainly tell us that there must have been a Designer. And both the matter and the motion of the universe point to the conclusion that there was ultimately a first cause. And the very fact that always there have been men who have believed there was a God indicates there is One. Where else would the idea have come from? And we recognize evil because we somehow perceive the good, and those perceptions bring us to an absolute good or truth.

But to understand or repeat any one of these beliefs or, indeed, all of them together, is not enough. Even if you knew their "big word" names, *cosmological, teleological, ontological,* or whatever, they are inadequate. When life caves in, you do not need reasons—you need comfort. You do not need some answers—you need *someone*. And Jesus does not come to us with an explanation—He comes to us with His presence.

We are always seeking the reason. We want to know why. Like Job, we finally want God to tell us just what is going on. Why do the good die young and the bad seem to live on forever? If the meek inherit the earth, why do the arrogant always seem to have the mineral rights? But God does not reveal His plan—He reveals Himself.

> He comes to us in so many ways—
> Warmth when we are cold,
> Fellowship when we are alone,
> Strength when we are weak,
> Peace when we are troubled,
> Courage when we are afraid,
> Songs when we are sad,
> And bread when we are hungry.

He is with us on our journeys. He is there when we are home. He sits with us at our table. He knows about funerals and weddings and commencements and hospitals and jails and unemployment and labor and laughter and rest and tears. He knows because He is with us—He comes to us again and again—until we can say, "It's You! It's You!"

For Jesus came to be experienced.

The insights and understandings from John 15 that follow in the book I have heard and learned. I have come to experience them as I put myself *in the scene* and as I sat in one of *His chairs* at *His table*. And they are things that have become mine because He has also come to sit at *my table* in one of *my chairs* and I have belatedly proclaimed, "It's You! It's You!"

Deep Right Field

I likes to be chose.

I have never been very big. I have consistently managed to be smaller than my contemporaries. One hundred forty-five pounds or so looks like it is going to be it. This is stretched over a frame that seems to be going from five-foot-ten and three-quarters back to five-foot-ten. I did get up to one hundred sixty-three pounds once. But I looked like a squirrel with acorns in its jaws. After my recent illness, Tom looked at my legs as I came out of the shower and called me Olive Oyl. In heaven, if I could be about six-foot-two and weigh around two hundred thirty-five, I would be willing to let someone else have my wings and I would probably throw in my harp to boot.

I was always a frail kid. My brother, John, would come home from school with childhood diseases like scarlet fever, the mumps, and measles and pass them on to me. He would have the three-week vacation from school to play in the yard, and I would be in bed for a month, while we were quarantined.

I can remember when we used to go out to recess in grammar school. The two biggest and strongest kids in the class were always made captains of the softball teams. Usually they made themselves the pitchers of the teams first, and then they picked the rest. One by one each kid was chosen—for athletic prowess, for friendship, for size, until finally everybody was on a team. Well—almost everybody.

"The game can't start until somebody takes Bob," the teacher would insist.

And one of the captains would kick the dust and say in disgust, "*We'll* take him."

And I was usually sent to play behind the right fielder. I don't think that I came up to bat until I was in the eighth grade. I wasn't too surprised to strike out then.

So, I likes to be "chosen."

And that is why these words of Jesus have such a lovely sound: "You did not choose me. I chose you."

The relationship of the shared life began when He chose me. It was not that I came upon Jesus Christ and, when I saw Him, something within me ran out to meet Him and, holding on to Him, begged Him to lift me out of myself and make me the person of my dreams. It was like this—He came upon me. His heart rushed out to me. He held on to me. He said He would make me the person I wanted to be. He saw me. He loved me and chose me. I did not find Him. He found me.

I heard a story the other day about being chosen. Someone asked another person if he would help him out on a project. He responded yes.

"I think it is only fair to tell you that you were my second choice," replied the first, maybe with more honesty than was called for.

"Well, that is all right," the willing worker said, "but just out of curiosity, who was your first choice?"

"Anybody," was the reply.

But I was not chosen as a replacement for someone who did not want to serve. I was not asked to play in the field that someone was already covering. He saw me, He called me, He selected me, He picked me, He singled me out, He decided on me, He opted for me, He fixed upon me, He determined in favor of me, He preferred me, He espoused me. *He chose me.*

He did not refuse me, He did not reject me, He did not repudiate me, He did not spurn me, He did not dismiss me, He did not exclude me. He did not ignore, disregard, cast away, throw aside, or leave me out. *He chose me.*

It was not obligatory, mandatory, required, called for, deserved, necessary, imperative, compulsory, or forced. *He just chose me.*

It was his open, voluntary, willful, selective, deliberate, intentional choice. *He chose me.*

Out of His devotion, fondness, adoration, tenderness, affection, attachment, emotion, sympathy, empathy, and love, *He just chose me.*

And that has made the difference.

I have come to the place where I dread to travel. When I know that I am going to be leaving home on Friday morning, I start getting homesick by Wednesday. On Thursday night Peg always asks if I am going to pack my suitcase before I go to bed. But just in case the thing is cancelled and I will not have to go, I wait until I get up on Friday to pack.

And Peggy will say to me, "Why are you going?"

"Well, I told them that I would come so I guess I will."

"Why did you tell them that you would come?"

"Because I was chosen."

In recent days it seems so very obvious that not only have I been chosen, but also protected and spared. We were playing the little "Why are you going?" game one night not too long ago, and Peggy said,

"You have to go."

"Why do I have to go?"

"You were chosen."

Now I know that the process by which God chooses men cannot be understood by looking at the *choosee*.

Some months ago, the Sunday school lesson was on the life of Judah. One of my good friends, Bob Hardin, was teaching, and I turned over to the thirty-eighth chapter of Genesis to follow along with him. He was having a bit of a time with Judah. In fact, he was not using much of the story at all. I read a little of it and began to understand why. It was not the sort of thing that you wanted to discuss in Sunday school—even in our enlightened adult group.

For one thing, Judah fathered a child with his widowed daughter-in-law. Well, you can excuse him a little bit because, in his defense, he did not know who she was. But if you have any suspicious streak in you at all, you will wonder who he *thought* she was.

But Judah was chosen. If you study Matthew's genealogy of Jesus, you will read:

> Abraham begat Isaac;
> Isaac begat Jacob;
> and Jacob begat Judah and his brothers.

And if you want to study the history of the same family in Luke's gospel, you will find Judah there, too, even though it's "backwards":

> Abinadab was the son of Ram,
> who was the son of Hezron,
> who was the son of Pharaz,
> who was the son of *Judah*.

There he is—coming and going—right there with all the heroes. It was hard for almost any heroines to make the list in those days. Maybe you wouldn't have included him. Maybe you do not understand why Judah was one of the ones chosen. But he was.

The last time the name of Judah is mentioned in the Bible is in the fifth chapter of Revelation. John was looking at a great book in the right hand of the one who was sitting on the throne. The book was sealed with seven seals. Nobody could open it. An angel asked in a loud voice, "Who is worthy to break the seals and open the book?" But nobody could open it. John began to weep because he wanted to see what was in it. And one of the elders said to him, "Do not weep; for the Lion out of the tribe of *Judah* will open the book and loose the seven seals."

He was chosen and the very choosing called him to what he could be.

I know that I am an improbable choice. You certainly cannot tell why I was chosen by observing me.

I have a very, very soft speaking voice. Coupled with that is a most disconcerting habit of lowering my voice even further when I get to something that I really want to emphasize. People often come up when I finish speaking and say to me, "I couldn't hear more than about half of what you said tonight."

"If you tell me the half you heard, I'll tell you the other half again," is my reply, and it usually turns out they can't even remember the half they heard.

I think of Moses who, incidentally, probably did talk loud. He was instructed by God to turn aside and see the burning bush. God did not tell him to scream and jump over the bush. He told him to take off his shoes because he was on holy ground. Holy ground makes me quieter than ever.

It is fun to observe people when I am first introduced and begin to speak. It seems that they are saying to themselves,

"Well, I can hardly hear him, so I will try to read his lips."

And then they notice that I do not move my lips very much, either. When you don't talk any louder than I do, you don't have to move your mouth very much. The words just sort of sneak out.

My speech teacher told me that I had lazy lips.

Further, I am a shy person who does not initiate conversations with strangers. I am not even noted for talking to those I do know. If you rode from here to Tallahassee beside me on a bus, I probably would not say much more than "Good morning" unless you happened to be sitting on my hat. To say the very least, I am not noted as a brilliant conversationalist.

I have already confided to you that I do not have a very impressive body. The other day somebody was saying, "Where is the speaker?" I didn't mind that too much because it was before the service. It happened again a little bit later and this time it was more humbling. Because this time I had just finished speaking.

And when you think of a rather shy little man with a quiet voice and lazy lips climbing on a plane to travel across the country to get up in front of a group of total strangers to talk to them—it does seem far-fetched.

I understand easily why it appears that I am both an implausible and illogical choice. I can only say that if it seems that way to those who know only a little about me, think how much more it is to *me* knowing all that *I* know about me. Fortunately my being chosen does not grow out of me—I am just a *choosee.*

The answer must be found in the heart of the *chooser.* It was not something in me that made Him call me. It was something in Him. It began in His love for me.

Our shared life with Him begins when he chooses us. And our being chosen begins in His love for us. *He is the initiator of this relationship.*

In one way this is a rejoicing kind of truth. It is like a serendipity or an extra. It is like boiled custard from the dairy, which is made only during the holidays between Thanksgiving and Christmas. You can't get it for your birthday in August. It is like a holiday or special-times-type truth and, at a retreat or in a particular service, it thrills us to think that He loves us.

In another, deeper way I am beginning to believe that this really is a foundation-type truth. There is the sense in which He cannot mean all He could or should to us, until we begin to fathom to some degree how much we mean to Him. All of our faith and love for Him is born in our belief in His trust and love for us.

Recently I have been reading a book by M. Scott Peck. The book, *The Road Less Traveled,* is subtitled "A New Psychology of Love, Traditional Values, and Spiritual Growth." Dr. Peck is an M.D. and practicing psychiatrist.

The last section of the book is on grace. In the first place I wondered why he should be using one of *our* words—grace. I don't make it a practice to borrow *his* terms and phrases, mostly because I can't pronounce them. To make it even worse he called it *amazing.* But really it bothered me that he was able to see and describe the operation of grace in so many ways and places that I had not even considered.

I think that my perception of grace is that it is something that comes to us as we request it, or as need arises within or around us. It is something special that is given for the moment. And I still think that is true. Dr. Peck, moreover, believes that grace is also ever-present and is the explanation for many things that we do not understand,

> We know very well why people become mentally ill. What we don't understand is why people survive the traumas of their lives as well as they do. We know exactly why certain people commit suicide. We don't know, within the ordinary concepts of casuality, why certain others don't commit suicide. All we can say is that there is a force, the mechanics of which we do not fully understand, that seems to operate routinely in most people to protect and foster their mental health even under the most adverse conditions.

To the miracles of health he adds the miracles of the unconscious, of serendipity, of the evolution of persons which defies the natural law of entropy. These miracles which he calls grace lead him to describe "the existence of a God who wants us to grow—*a God who loves us.*"

Because grace comes to us outside the bounds of the ordinary course of things, it amazes us. Peck writes that *amazing* and *grace* do indeed go together.

His final few pages are subtitled "The Welcoming of Grace" and he concludes,

> We do not come to grace, grace comes to us. We may seek it not, yet it will find us. . . . The universe, this stepping-stone, has been laid down to prepare a way for us. But we ourselves must step across it, one by one. Through grace we are helped not to stumble and through grace *we know we are being welcomed.* What more can we ask?

And this belief in the goodness of God and in His constant expression of this goodness to us is indeed a fundamental and bedrock belief.

A lot of times in retreats, the Friday night session will open with skits and games. In a burst of hospitality Peg and I are often asked to be in the skits so that the people can get acquainted with us quickly. There is nothing like making a fool of yourself to break the ice. In a retreat in Colorado, Peg was the rich rancher's lovely daughter and her entire part consisted of two words, "Who, me?" By the time she had repeated these words in Southern drawl a few dozen times during the drama, she was known and loved by all.

At a recent retreat one of the games was musical chairs. It got louder and more rambunctious in uncanny proportion to the ever-decreasing number of chairs. Finally one person was on the floor, the winner was in the last chair, and the rest of us were yelling.

Sometimes I talk to people who seem to think that God is playing musical chairs—like, every so often, He just stops the music. There isn't any rhyme or reason or fairness to it—it's just whether you were around the corner when it stopped. And whether or not you can now beat some big guy to the last chair. And every time the music stops, somebody has to drop out. No wonder they don't like God. I wouldn't like Him either if I thought He was playing musical chairs with us.

But He has a chair for everybody. If you end up on the floor, it won't be because He didn't have a seat for you. It will be because you won't sit in it. And He plays the music on and on and on to give you every opportunity to go clear around again and again until you find your place.

It is not always easy to believe this about yourself. It is almost easier to believe it about others. You know yourself too well to see how this could be. But the shared life can only begin to grow in you as you start to understand how very much He cares for you. It is important what you think He thinks about you.

As long as you feel that you can only hope
that He isn't displeased or pouting
or mad or gone.

As long as you believe that He is
saying or feeling about you,
"Oh no, not again!"
"Look at that!"
"Will he ever get that right?"
"She always does that."
As long as *your failure* causes you
to doubt *His faithfulness*,
You're looking at the *choosee*.
Only when you can realize He is
looking at you and
smiling with you and
thanking the Father for you,
Will you begin to find
the love there is
in the heart of the *Chooser*.

I was reading the other day how a lady of long ago came to recognize the love God in Christ has for us. It was in a volume in the series, *The Classics of Western Spirituality*. It was my introduction to a fourteenth-century solitary named Julian of Norwich. Very little is known about her except for what one may learn or deduce from the book she wrote.

She lived her solitary, enclosed life in the late fourteenth and early fifteenth centuries, probably in a cell adjoining the parish church of St. Julian, in Conisford at Norwich. The church still stands, and the cell itself, which was destroyed during World War II, has since been rebuilt.

It is not known where she was born, or who or what her family or her religious history were, or when she died. But she does tell us that she received revelations from God on May 13, 1373, when she was thirty and a half years old. If she had not believed she was divinely commanded to write down the record of her visions, her name might have been no more today than one among the thousands who lived in medieval England as solitaries for the love of God.

Her writing centers around the prayers that she earnestly prayed and the revelations that came to her as answers "by bodily vision, by words formed in her understanding, and by spiritual vision."

She desired to have recollection of Christ's Passion so that she might see what He had suffered for her. She longed to be *in the scene.*

She prayed that His pains might be her pains so that she might be led into a deeper longing for God. Praying for understanding and compassion, she suddenly saw the red blood trickling down from under the crown, flowing freely and copiously, a living stream, as if it were at the time the crown of thorns was thrust down upon His head. And after a time she saw Him as He died. And His face changed as death took hold of His body. As her eyes were fixed upon Christ on the cross, the expression on His face changed from sorrow and pain to joy. The change in His countenance suddenly filled her with joy and gladness also.

And the Lord put a question to her. "Are you well satisfied that I have suffered for you?"

"Yes, good Lord, all my thanks to you, good Lord, blessed may you be!" was her answer.

And then *He* said to her, "If you are satisfied, I am satisfied. It is a joy and a bliss and an endless delight to me that ever I suffered my passion for you. And if I could suffer more, I would."

And in these words, Julian saw that if Christ would be willing to die as often as once for every man if need be, just as He did once for all men, His love would never let Him rest until He had done it. For Jesus has great joy in all He has done for our salvation. We are

His bliss, we are His reward, we are His honor, we are His crown, we are His joy.

I think I have been a longtime believer in the love of God as expressed to us through Christ. This divine love has always seemed to me to be a fixed attitude or set of mind. Unchanging, eternal, redemptive, constant—it radiates from Him. But Jesus used a word here with His disciples that throws open to me a whole new dimension for thought and celebration. The word is *joy*. In the setting of these last hours with His disciples, Jesus is telling them how much they mean to Him. He is saying these things to them that their joy may be full and so that He may have joy in theirs. They are His joy.

It is not strange to associate the word *joy* with Jesus, for it is a quality that just seems to be inherent in His mission and message from the Father. He brings joy, He gives joy, He radiates joy, He bestows joy on all those who trust Him and walk in His ways. These are His ways, and we say and sing and celebrate them. We know how He makes our hearts glad.

But here He also speaks about the thing that makes His heart glad. All the while we have been content to accept joy as something we receive from Him. Now hear Him saying that joy is something that comes *to Him* because *of us*.

What is it that makes Him joyful in this hour of separation in an Upper Room? As He looks back across the long years of preparation and the short years of public ministry, what is it that makes Him smile? As He looks now across the last few hours to His death, what is it that makes Him conclude that His has been a useful, worthwhile, joyful life?

It was His *joy* in men, given to Him by the Father. There wasn't anything else—they were all He had. But they were enough—they were His joy.

One of the young men who works at the company is Phil Johnson. It was the association with people like him that made it so hard to resign. Phil is a talented producer, artist, musician, husband and father, and a warm Christian. One of his songs is called "When I Say Jesus." It expresses an inspirational thought about what the name of Jesus means to us and what that name has the power to do for us.

One afternoon I was talking to him a little about the song and he told me he wanted to write another song with a parallel truth, but he was afraid no one would understand it. I asked him what he would name the song. "When I Say Phil," was his reply.

I'm not sure we would understand it. Or believe it if we did. It is easy for us to know the wealth of meaning and grace that comes to us when we say His name—Jesus.

What a flood of memories and recollections is opened up at the thought of His name. It does not take long to look back across your life and think of all the various times and places you have breathed that precious name. At first it was only in the hard places—when your ma died, when the baby was sick, or when you lost your job. Gradually, though, He became interwoven into the celebrations and the good times as well and His name began to be the invocation and benediction of all your days. And as Phil wrote:

When I say "Master,"
My sorrows disappear.
When I say "Father,"
He drives away my fears;
When I say "Saviour,"
My blinded eyes can see,
When I say "Jesus,"
He speaks peace to me!

Property of
David & Becky Warren

It is not hard to sing Phil's song and to know what happens in you and for you when you say Jesus. But can you believe that He speaks your name with the same depth and feeling that you speak His? Can you realize that He, too, looks back across the years to the day He chose you and rejoices in what you have come to mean to Him as you have walked together?

My son Tom is an avid student of expression mannerisms, voice inflections, and all the other things that make each of us unique. As a result, he can mimic almost anyone he has been around. And as soon as he goes into one of his impressions, you realize that although you hadn't noticed it before—that is just the way that person is.

The other night at the supper table he was giving us a little rundown on the faculty at school. Some of them I had not met. But I knew them when I did. Patrick, who goes to the same school, knew them all and nearly doubled up with laughter.

Tom stopped his stories to say that he loved to see Patrick laugh. When we asked him why, he gave us a description and a demonstration of Patrick's face as it moves from seriousness to mirth.

"First, his eyes brighten and his eyebrows widen and then his nostrils quiver and his mouth begins to spread upward and outward at the corners until he passes the point of no return and laughs without control."

We really have no way of knowing what Jesus actually looked like. The only way we can envision Him physically is from one of the various paintings that have been rendered of Him. Even then, though, it is only the artist's conception of Jesus, whether it be youthful, sad, vigorous, solemn, or happy. Probably none of them are just like Him. The famous picture of the Last Supper didn't happen just like it appears on the canvas. It looks posed to me, like the artist told everyone who wanted in the picture to get on one side of the table.

Still, it helps to see a face. And when you are praying and looking up to Him or when you feel Him looking down on you, He very likely appears to you much like your favorite picture of Him.

Can you close your eyes and visualize His face? Now, speak His name and listen as He says yours back to you. And as He is saying your name, can you see His eyes brighten, His eyebrows widen, His nostrils quiver, and His mouth begin to spread upward and outward until His face is bathed in smiles that come from deep within His heart?

Remember, the shared life began when He chose you, and He chose you because He loves you.

Rivers and Ponds

Some time ago, my pastor, Millard Reed, called and asked if I would speak at the church on a coming Sunday. He was going to be away.

"Well, the last time I spoke, I didn't do so well," I said, remembering that a prophet doesn't have much honor in his own country. More than a hundred miles from home I'm an expert, and more than two hundred and thirty, I'm a *gospel hero*.

"That's what I heard and I thought that I would give you another chance," was his reply.

Overwhelmed by his confidence, I could not turn him down. When I did get up to speak that Sunday morning, I asked the people present not to tell on me this time. I figured if he really wanted to know how well I did, he could just stay and take his chances with the rest of them.

It was to be the beginning of my study of these verses in the fifteenth chapter of John. Some of the verses began to say things to me that I had not heard before. I was reading from the New English Bible, or "Neb," as Tom calls it. My reading an "alternate" translation sometimes alarms people, but I hasten to tell them that I still pray in the King James.

One of the phrases that gripped my attention was a part of the fourth verse: "Dwell in me, as I dwell in you." I was familiar, as you are, with these words as they are translated in the King James Version, "Abide in me, and I in you."

I am not a Greek scholar. I am not certain just how this word may be translated from the Greek either *and* or *as*. But in English I suddenly saw a difference of such rich significance that I am still rejoicing in its meaning.

The word *and* is a conjunction. It carries the meaning of *as a result* or *in consequence of*. The even shorter word *as* is an adverb and its meaning is *to the same degree*, or *in the same manner* or *since*.

Before, I had been reading *and*. I had been hearing it just about the same as I heard it in the verse, "Seek, *and* you will find." I was understanding that *I* was to do something—namely live in Him, and then, *as a result, in consequence of, because of what I had done*, He would reciprocate by living in me.

But when I read *as*, I began to hear Him saying something far different. Now He was saying that I could live in Him *in the same manner* that He was living in me.

When I read *and*, it began with *me*. I caused Him to act.

if I—then He
when—then He
as I—then He
abide in me *and* I in you.

When I read *as*, it began with *Him*. He enables me to act.

He has—I can
He is—I can
in the same way—I can
live in me *as* I live in you.

And I have found that things which come from Him and reach down to me are always better than those things that start with me and reach up to Him. He is not only the initiator of this shared life because He chose me. I am beginning to see, also, that *He is its character and its strength*.

A few weeks before I was to begin my sophomore year in college, I came down with asthma. This was a common occurrence for me in the fall. At the last moment the decision was made to try the climate on the West Coast. Almost before I knew it I found myself some two thousand miles from home enrolled in Pasadena Nazarene College. I was quite homesick. I do not think homesickness is fatal. But I am not sure I would have made it had it not been for the Shinglers.

Bertha and Lewis are longstanding friends of the family. They went to college with both my parents and Peg's. In fact, Lewis and Peg's dad, Wally, were roommates.

The Shinglers and their children did their very best to help me overcome my initial loneliness. Nancy and Art were both young enough to be sufficiently impressed by a college sophomore. They all made me feel at home with meals, sightseeing trips, gifts, and love. One of the gifts was a devotional book by Andrew Murray entitled *Abide in Christ*.

I still have that little book. I treasure it, both because it was given to me by the Shinglers and because of its contents. I have shared experiences down across the years with this book.

The cover shows its age. Back and forth across the

country it has moved with me from study to study, pastorate to pastorate, and home to home. It has been nearly flattened from being packed again and again with its bigger and heavier neighbors on the shelf. Somewhere, sometime, somebody used it as a coaster and the ring of a pop bottle is etched across its face. The title has long since disappeared from the backbone—a victim to wear, climate, silverfish, and age. But I recognize it when I see it on the shelf because it is an old friend.

That book is also an old adversary. Until recently only the first few pages were marked. You can always tell how far I've read in a book by the markings. The ribbon was between pages twenty-two and twenty-three. Many times I had turned to it for insight and inspiration, but I always seemed to put it aside after those first few pages. It was not that it did not say anything to me. The problem was that it always said too much.

I recall more than once turning to it as a young pastor. Every Monday I would determine that I would complete the task of sermon preparation early. Sometimes I was still making the same resolution on Thursday. And sometimes, Saturday night would find me in the study long after the family had gone to bed. I would be looking for the idea that would free my mind from the paralysis of fear and lead me to a message. I know your pastor never does this, but just the same, it wouldn't hurt to breathe a little prayer for him before you go to bed on Saturday night—maybe he's working on sermons for Sunday week.

At such times I often picked up *Abide in Christ* and I would always be impressed with the things it had to say. But I could not find a way to use the truths written so beautifully. It was like trying to write a check on a bank where I didn't have an account. I would put the book back in its place on the shelf. And I would resolve anew that I would learn to live in Him acceptably *and* then He would have to come and live in me, bringing to me all the grace of which Murray spoke. Then I could preach about the shared life with the ring of witness and authority and with His glory on my face.

One of the few things I did identify with in the book was Murray's description of the Israelite wanderings in the wilderness: "ever on the way, never very far, and always coming short."

The problem was always the same. *I* was going to make myself a worthy place for Him to dwell. *I* was going to paint the living room and straighten the closets, and *I* was going to mow the yard and clean out the garage and fix the faucets, and then *He* would choose to come and live in my worthiness.

And for a long time now *I* have tried to lead an adequate Christian life. But *I* am not adequate.

These are hard words for me to write, because I am afraid someone will say that what I need is some new *crisis* experience. Or worse yet, they will wonder if I ever even had an old one. But I have had all the *crisis* experiences that one is supposed to have—some of them more than once. What I really need is a *daily* experience, a type of life that is lived through His living presence in me.

I have yielded and I have sincerely committed and I do believe. I was dedicated as an infant, converted as a teen-ager, baptized, sanctified, called, and ordained in the church. Each of those experiences has been a place of high purpose and meaning for me. But my life does not always maintain itself on those plains of hope and expectation. He must meet my life at all the other places, from fear to boredom as well. To be able to meet life with courage and equanimity, to maintain steadfastness and presence of mind in the situations of life—these have long been desires of my heart. But *I* am not adequate.

We all have mornings when we know that this is going to be one day when He is going to be proud of us. He is lucky to have somebody like us on His side this time. We are ready. We are prepared. But something goes wrong. Something happens for which we are not ready. Someone comes along we were not prepared to see. And we end the day with the pillow over our face, with tears in our eyes and chagrin in our hearts.

Sam Keen, in his book *To A Dancing God,* describes more than one of us when he writes of his discovery that "the sanctity required of me was not within the range of my willpower."

After a while one gets to know oneself pretty well. It seems that on the pilgrimage of my life a trio of troublemakers has always been a part of me—the inability to discipline myself; a kind of critical, scathing temper; and an inexhaustible stream of impure thoughts. If I could be free of these, I could become myself.

So it is right at this place that the implications of the difference between *and* and *as* comes to me. I hear Him saying to me, "I did not choose you because you were adequate. I did not choose you because you were strong. I did not even choose you because I ever thought you were going to become adequate. I chose you and I have come to live in you, and you can live in Me because I am living in you."

For several years now I have made some attempt to maintain some kind of journal of my life. In high school I would have called it a diary, but now I prefer to call it a journal in the manner of John Wesley or some other great person. I believe that keeping a journal is an excellent way of putting one in touch with oneself, although I am not a particularly good example of a journal-keeper. I usually have a pretty good daily record of my Januarys and Februarys, but Marches, Aprils, and Mays tend to be weekly. And by fall, I am on the quarter system.

To be really effective in this self-discovery process, you should be very honest in the things that you enter in your journal. Feelings, accomplishments, failures, and the reasons for them should be straightforward and transparent. Occasionally, you have the feeling that maybe somewhere and sometime, someone will be reading this historic work and you want them to know how noble you really were, so you tend to be *careful.* After all, you want them to remember you at your best. You want to lock the journal up, but you also want to leave the keys on the desk in case anyone did want to read it and brag on you for the forthrightness of your character.

Here and there in my writings, though, there are enough bits of honesty to surprise even me with the range of my moods and resolve. The fluctuations of my feelings about myself and my opportunities and cares are frequent and wide.

It is hard to believe that the person who notes, "I should make my best contributions this year . . . leadership established . . . confidence of friends and family and many other things are at the strongest focus of my life"—is the same person who just a few pages later also comments: "Haven't performed well lately . . . cannot resolve in my mind why I am so negative . . . I should have a quiet strength . . . somehow it eludes me. And when people think I have it, I feel even worse." How can I be so filled with peace and motivation one day and so characterized by questions and doubt the next?

I am looking again at these two little words, *and*

and *as*. And I am coming to see that they are telling me this shared life is not grounded on the performance recorded in my daily journal. It is not built on the foundations of my constancy. It does not find its nourishment in the depths of my devotion. It finds its strength in Him.

Who always loves? Who always cares? Who always helps? Who always comes? Who always believes? Who always hopes? Who is always the same—yesterday, today, forever? He does; He has; He is; He will; He can.

One of the reasons I always bogged down so early in Murray's book was the truth of the very first devotional. You can see I didn't get too far. It is a study of two invitations of Jesus. The first is from Matthew 11:28: "Come unto me." The other is from John 15:4: "Abide in me." I could handle the 11:28 okay. It was the 15:4 that eluded me. Now I believe that these twin calls of Christ are to be read together and they are saying to us, "Come to me and stay with me."

This was His purpose from the very beginning when He first called us to Himself. He did not call us to refresh us for a few hours or days after our conversion with the joy of His great love and deliverance, only to send us forth to wander alone in the same places we had always been—only now, with the added burden of obedience to Him. He did not beckon us to a short-lived blessedness that is enjoyed only in special times of earnestness and commitment but somehow has a way of fading when we return to the duties in which the greater part of our lives must be spent.

The same tenderness and compassion that He used in calling you to *come* surrounds and pervades His invitation to *live*. And the same power that brought you to Him must be what enables you to live in Him.

S. D. Gordon is one of the great devotional writers of another day. His series of books, *Quiet Talks*, is a treasury of rich truth. Some of Gordon's books have been reprinted, and recently I bought his *Quiet Talks On Prayer.* In this volume on prayer he writes about power in our lives:

> There is one inlet of power in the life—anybody's life—any kind of power; just one inlet—the Holy Spirit. He is power. There are five outlets of power: five avenues through which this One within shows Himself and reveals His power. First: through the life, *what we are.* Second: through the lips, *what we say.* Third: through our service, *what we do.* Fourth: through our money, *what we do not keep, but loosen out for God.* And fifth, through our prayer, *what we claim* in Jesus' name.

As one who ministers the truth and as an observer of others who are engaged in this task, I think that preachers really have two chief things they are trying to do. The first of these is to get people to *give all to Jesus.*

We go at this in a variety of ways. Sometimes we try to reason with you. If that doesn't work, we may try sentiment. If that isn't effective, we may sing the last verse of "Almost Persuaded" a few more times until the words, "Sad, sad, that bitter wail, almost but lost," do their work. We are not above scaring you if we have to. We just want you to *give* your all to Jesus. It's not always easy to do, or to get others to do.

But the second task is harder than the first, and we ministers are far less successful in it. And that is to get people *to receive all from Jesus.*

We have all read the little motto that says,

> Life is God's gift to me;
> What I do with it is my gift to Him.

I think I understand the intent of these words, don't you? They strike a responsive chord in my heart. Still, I think I have a deep disagreement with them. I think they indicate a common mistake we make in attempting to live in Him.

As Gordon put it so graphically: what you are, what you say, what you do, what you give, are indeed important, but not nearly so important as what you claim—what you receive. The life in Christ is not a self-improvement course. True—it will take your effort and your will and your diligence. But when all of that has been expended, one begins to realize that what it really takes is a strength beyond his own. He opened His arms to *call* you to Himself and He opened His heart to *welcome* you there. And now you must believe that He opens all of Himself to *keep* you there.

A couple of falls ago, Peg and I went out to Oregon where I was to speak in Sunday services in Salem. H. B. London, Jr. is pastor of the congregation where I was speaking. We have come to look forward to being with him and Bev.

I don't really like to go into a church to speak for just one day. You just have a few minutes and they go by so quickly. Almost before you know it, the people are out and on their way home. In that context I don't ever think I can do or say much that is in any way life-changing. I need to know at least a few people and a few of them need to know me. It takes people a while to get used to me and to learn to read my lips.

I told Pastor London this, and he said he would give me plenty of time. And he did. He also said the men in the church would be up in the woods together on Friday night and Saturday, and I could come up in the afternoon and have a chance to get acquainted. That way I would know some names and faces—I usually know more faces than I do names—and some of the people would know me, at least enough to pray for me. They would realize that I wasn't *bringing the service* with me. And I could share my hopes for the day and ask them what they were expecting. Then we could begin to pray in a *united* way.

On Saturday afternoon H. B. met us at the airport and we dropped Peg at the motel. In an hour or so I was speaking to the men in a lovely lodge in the mountains. When it was over and most of the men had drifted outside to wait for supper, H. B. said, "Let's go for a walk."

We started down the path through the forest. In a little while, after a fork or two in the trail, we came to a lovely mountain stream. The water was as cold and clear as it must have been the day God created it—before the Communists put fluoride in it. It was a beautiful moment as the late afternoon sunlight filtered through the trees and we both stood silent, thinking our own thoughts. We watched the river dancing in the light and singing its way across the rocks. I thought of words from Genesis: "And God said, 'Let there be lights in the vault of heaven to separate day from night, and let them serve as signs . . . for festivals'" (Gen. 1:14 NEB).

All too soon, H.B. said, "We'd better start back or we'll miss supper." Now H.B. is a leader among men and so when the path narrowed, I would fall in behind him. And the leader of men took the wrong path. After a while, we heard the dining hall bell being rung—but it was way across from where we were. He suggested we cut across toward the sound of the bell. I was thinking to myself: *You got lost on the path.*

But we started through the underbrush and we climbed up a little bank. When we got to the top, we realized that we were standing on an earthen dam that had been pushed up with a bulldozer. The water impounded behind it was green and stagnant. There was no music or dancing light. Just a motionless, lifeless, polluted pond.

Men make ponds. God makes rivers. Men dig wells. God makes springs. And our living in Him is not to be likened to a pond which we have bulldozed and scratched out of the hillsides of our lives. It was meant to be like streams of cool, clear, living water that He alone can bring.

As long as you think you are adequate or that you are supposed to be adequate, you will live your life within the bounds of your own grace and strength. Go ahead! Roll up your sleeves, clench your fist, bite your lip, grit your teeth, weep on your pillow, push up another pond, dig another shallow well.

No combination, however earnest, of *I pledge, I will, I must, I resolve, I commit* can make you what you want to be. It will not begin in you and reach upward to Him. It must start in Him and come down to you.

Men make ponds. God makes rivers. Rivers of freshness and cleanness that bubble and bless and make us what we never dreamed we could be.

"Live in me *as* I live in you."

Home-Home

Every now and then I find myself doing something my dad taught me when I was a kid. Something I vowed I would never do when I grew up and was on my own. Like nearly every other boy in the neighborhood, I had made up my mind that when I had my own home it was going to have a green concrete yard. I don't know why I won't go ahead and admit that I am more and more like my dad everyday. I guess it is because I would have to acknowledge that he was right about most things.

For instance, he not only loved to garden—he loved to garden early in the morning. My brother, John T., and I used to argue over who was going to deliver the morning paper route and who was going to the garden with Dad to chop weeds.

But this spring I found myself planting a garden. What is worse, I like to get up early in the morning to work in it. And, just like my dad, I began with thorough research of seed catalogs. I ordered every one I could find advertised. For awhile I thought just reading the catalogs would get the gardening out of my system, but it only increased my anticipation of spring. I made out the order and eagerly awaited the arrival of the package like a kid. Well, really, I was waiting on the box from Burpee like a *dad.* And I read every magazine and book on how to raise vegetables I could find while I waited.

Finally, the seeds came and at last the weather was warm enough to turn the soil and plant my garden. I guess I should say *gardens* because the rabbits and the cutworms quietly devoured the first one while we took a trip with the kids on their spring break. I'm watching this one like a full-time scarecrow. Peg asked if I were going to plant any onions, and I told her I didn't think so because I hate rabbits with bad breath.

But if I never bring anything into the house from the garden for the table, it will still have been worth it because I always come in with wonder in my heart. There is something about a seed.

"Peter, the Editor," as he signs his name at the bottom of his column in the magazine, *House and Porch Gardens,* was writing about seeds one day. His words, too, are filled with fascination:

> For instance, some seeds recently germinated in my office. Seeds germinate in these offices all the time and very little is made of the event. Germination is just a normal, predictable result of keeping a seed warm and moist. For some reason, however, it occurred to me that seeds make just about everything else seem trivial. As I was in my desk, looking at the first ugly leaf poking through the soil, and a peapod, it seemed to me that what was happening was important beyond my ability to observe and understand. Seeds are simple, but they are complex. They are common and plain, but secretly,

> they contain flowers. Seeds are ugly, there's no doubt about it. They're monotonous, but they are wonderful. Seeds wander. . . . Seeds carry oak and walnut trees around. Seeds are miniature plants, bundled for winter . . . seeds are very encouraging creatures that persist in their labors until they succeed, no matter what. No matter how many fail . . . almost anything can happen in the plant world as long as a few seeds keep trying . . . no matter how unlikely or difficult a horticultural event may seem, a seed could do it, if it wished.

And so I took those tiny seeds, mailed to me in a box from Iowa, and put them into the earth. I think I planted some of them too deep and some of them too shallow. I'm sure, now, that I planted some of them too thick and I planted some of them too thin. By all odds I probably planted most of them upside down. They are not marked "This Side Up," you know. But the secret to their life is not written on the outside—it is within them.

Outside forces like rookie farmers, obese rabbits, and lumberjack cutworms may torment the roots and harass the stalk. But with whatever freedom we allow the poor seed to live its own life, its built-in energies and knowledge never give up. It knows what it is supposed to be doing and it does it. It knows what it is supposed to be and it becomes it. It knows the rules of life and it lives them. It goes about its business of bursting forth in root and stem and fruit. Life, as the seed knows, is not some proper combination of external forces and factors; it springs from within.

Howard Thurman tells us that this is the integrity of life, ". . . this is the miracle, the shaping of matter from within: the materializing of vitality."

And I believe it is of this *inwardness* of life that Jesus is speaking when he says ". . . apart from me . . .

nothing" His words do not simply mean *without His help*. We do not neglect to ask Him for His help. In fact, most of the time, it is embarrassing to hear ourselves pray for *our* church, *our* families, *our* missionaries, *our* leaders, *our* plans, and *our* "*ours*." The meaning is deeper than His help. It is beyond asking for His aid for our projects and plans.

His words are about *being separated from Him*. He is speaking here of sources and citadels and springs.

He is asking us these questions:
What waters you?
What feeds you?
Where does the nourishment
of your life come from?
What is it which lets you go back to sleep
when you are awakened in the night?
What gives you the courage to get up
and go on as if you never fell?
What really makes you smile?
What gives you hope?
What brings you peace?
What do you count on to help you be
a husband, wife, or parent?
Who is it that keeps you from being alone
although you are by yourself?

When He says "apart from me," He is not just talking about what we do. He is asking us where we live.

For several years Peggy and I casually looked for a place around Middle Tennessee or Kentucky that we could use for small retreats. It had to be reasonably close to home and big enough to divide into sleeping spaces. To be honest with you, we found a place and then discovered maybe we didn't need it as badly as we had thought we did. But that is another story.

The place we found is a lovely log house up near

Russellville, Kentucky. Russellville has its own claim to history. The oldest bank up there is the first bank that Jesse James ever held up. I tried to get a little money out of that bank myself, but it always seemed that the banker had the gun.

Anyway, when we were looking at the house, we wanted the kids to like it. Tom and Patrick showed some enthusiasm and probably would have been willing to move up there. Leigh's a sentimental girl, though, and she didn't even want to look at some place that might even remotely compete for the name "home." She was plenty happy right where she was.

Finally, I got her to ride up there with me and look at the house. I pointed out the great stone fireplaces, one of which was in what could have been her room, and the beauty of the logs. We walked through the wooded acreage and I finally asked her,

"Do you like it at all?"

"It's okay."

"Well, would you come up here with us if it was ours?"

"I guess so," was her begrudging answer.

We were quiet a minute and then she said to me, "Just as long as we all realize that when it is time to go home, we go to our *home-home*."

And I understood what she was feeling so deeply.

I think her words *home-home* tell us a little of what Jesus was meaning when He said, ". . . apart from me . . ." He wants to be our *home-home*—

not our summer place,
not a vacation retreat,
not somewhere we go from time to time,
but the place we are
when we want to be
home-home.

He is saying that we will never be at home until we are at home in Him. For there is no life apart from the source of life and He is the source. When we are severed from the vine, we are severed from life itself. He alone is the one who can ". . . be an inner spring always welling up for eternal life."

Generally, our attempt to find remedies for life—our needs, our wants, our fulfillment—are made from the outside in. Robert Frost tells us this again in his poignant way in his poem, "The Investment."

> Over back where they speak of life as staying
> ("You couldn't call it living, for it ain't"),
> There was an old, old house renewed with paint,
> And in it a piano loudly playing.
>
> Out in the plowed ground in the cold a digger,
> Among unearthed potatoes standing still,
> Was counting winter dinners, one a hill,
> With half an ear to the piano's vigor.
>
> All that piano and new paint back there,
> Was it some money suddenly come into?
> Or some extravagance young love had been to?
> Or old love on an impulse not to care—
>
> Not to sink under being man and wife,
> But get some color and music out of life?

And so it is with most of us—we live as if life itself was on the outside. As if brighter paint and louder music will bring to us those meanings and joys which we so desperately long for and need.

It is probably quite significant that one of the business phenomena of our day is an industry that has come to be known by the speed and efficiency with which the product is dispensed rather than by the quality of the product itself. We do not speak of the nourishing food business, or the gracious dining food business, or the economical food business—it is the *fast food* business. Never mind the taste, much less the nutrition. It is in a pretty box and, most of all, it can be served to us in a hurry.

And the society in which we live today would have us believe, or at least hope, that life will be okay if we can just get it packaged right and served to us on the run. But wrappings and to-go windows have very little to do with the quality of life itself. The real processes of life take place somewhere deep within us. For within all of us there is a wish for meaning. It may only come occasionally, like a flash of summer lightning, but it comes. Though we may sometimes doubt the quality of spiritual bread, we can't kid ourselves that we are not hungry.

> There is a sense of wholeness at the core of man
> That must abound in all he does;
> That marks with reverence his every step;
> That has its way when all else fails;
> That wearies all our evil things;
> That warms the depth of frozen fears
> Making friends of foe,
> Making love of hate,
> And lasts beyond the living and the dead,
> Beyond the goals of living, the ends of war!
> This man seeks through all his years:
> To be complete and of one piece, within, without.

I have two observations that I think I am ready to make about one's quest for life. The first of them is that such a search for life and its attendant meaning is *a journey on which you will come to find yourself.* It is *an inward journey.*

Elizabeth O'Connor is one of those people who influences her generation in a compelling way. I have never met her except for one short telephone conversation. In just a few moments she turned aside a request I was making for her to speak; further impressed me with her devotion to her purposes and calling; and inquired a little about a voice on the phone that she had never heard before. I have also been moved by her books, in which she has some significant things to say about life. Here are some of her words:

> Each of us is the artist of his own life. The materials we are given to work with, the conditions we work under and what happens to us, are part of the drama of what we shall do with our lives. But materials and conditions and events are not, in themselves, the determining factors. Whether a man arrives or does not arrive at his destiny—the place that is peculiarly his—depends on whether or not he finds the Kingdom within and hears the call to wholeness—or holiness, as another might say. The man who hears the call is chosen. He does not have to scramble for a place in the scheme of things. He knows there is a place which is his and that he can live close to the One who will show it to him.

One of the folk heroes at our house is John Denver. The kids have played his records and sung his songs until they are a part of many lovely memories and happy moments. My eyes still fill with tears when I hear him sing songs like "Poems and Prayers and Promises." He has captured in the words of his songs deep meanings that are true for all of us.

He has begun to do this with his camera as well. Not so long ago he was in New York City for the opening of an exhibition of some of his photographs of Colorado. In a television interview he was asked, "What would you like for people to say about you when you are gone?"

After a moment or two, he answered, "I would like for them to say, I think, *he became himself*."

The task of becoming one's own self is probably more difficult than any of us imagine. A part of the problem is that we are not always so sure whether we are supposed to be radishes or tomatoes or nasturtiums or thistles. And it is further complicated by the fact that we can choose which one of those we would like to try to be. And even worse, we are *all* of them *some* of the time. But *one* of them is us.

Thomas Merton, who lived his life on this same journey to find himself, wrote in *New Seeds of Contemplation:*

> A tree gives glory to God by being a tree. . . . The more a tree is like itself the more it is like him. . . . For me to be a saint means to be myself. Trees and animals have no problem. God makes them what they are. . . . With us it is different. . . . We can be ourselves or not, as we please. We are at liberty to be real, or to be unreal. We may be true or false, the choice is ours. We may wear now one mask and now another, and never, if we so desire, appear with our own face. But we cannot make these choices with impunity. . . . If we have chosen the way of falsity we must not be surprised that truth eludes us when we finally come to need it!

The tragedy that gradually befalls us is not that others do not know who we are—it is that *we* do not know who we are. And we spend our days knocking on every door hoping that we will find the one that has our name on it.

When Peg and I were married, someone very close to us painted a picture for us to hang in our living room. It was, needless to say, the only original oil painting that we had and, because it was done especially for us, we were very proud of it. Later on we were visiting in the home of some mutual friends and were somewhat surprised to see a painting of the same scene done by our artist. It happened two other times. So now there were four of the fall forest scenes that we had seen. The painting was not quite as special as it had been before. Still, it had been done in love and it must have taken hours and hours, and it was well done.

But the thing that finally kept us from putting the picture up again the next time we moved happened one afternoon in a furniture store. There, on the wall, with dozens of other "printed paintings" was our scene. *Our friend had painted someone else's picture.*

Many of us will never be truly happy or fulfilled because we never succeed in becoming ourselves. We never get around to being the particular person or painter that we were intended to be. We live our lives *painting someone else's picture*. We are not willing to take our palette and our paints and our brush and go to the mountain or the forest or the sea and labor until we have captured its beauty on our canvas. We only see their majesty through someone else's eyes and with the strokes of their brush.

Still, the quality of the seed, the life principle within us, the inner vitality never rests until it has made itself known and has been recognized and allowed to become that which it was supposed to be.

It is true that we may ignore this call to life from time to time, but it will make itself heard again. It is as Carl Jung wrote, "The aspect of ourselves which we sacrifice in the attainment of a given object of our lives is reborn alive and comes back after many years, knife in hand, demanding to sacrifice that which sacrificed it." Because, like the tiny seed, hidden somewhere within us is what we are supposed to be and what we are supposed to do.

One of the errors that we often make in this search for self is our failure to realize that the road which leads to self and the road which Jesus travels are one and the same. And the journeys that we make in other directions, away from Him, are also trips that take us away from ourselves. For some reason we think that real life is away from home and the Father and, like the prodigal son, we leave only to find that we are leaving behind the things which gave us life.

Not too long ago a couple who have been our good friends decided that they could not be a couple any longer. And so they divided their accumulated goods and the children, divorced, and went their separate ways. The cause, at least the one that was most visible to those of us who knew them, was an inability on the husband's part to live up to the vows of faithfulness, thus denying the marriage its very foundations of sanctity. He readily acknowledged that probably only God could provide the strength that he was unable to find within himself. But he could not or would not ask for God's help. Somehow, it is in his mind that in return for His help, God will want him to be somebody he does not want to be. He cannot believe that what he truly wants for himself and what God truly wants for him are one and the same. And my friend, though he might not see it now, is not just avoiding God—he is avoiding himself as well.

It is true, I believe, that when we come to ourselves; when we write our book or sing our song or fill our place; when we paint our own picture, we will have also come close to Jesus, for we will have begun to discover the life that He put within us. Thus it is also true that the closer we come to Him, the closer we will be coming to life itself.

One of the first ways we begin to make our journey toward Him who is life is in the manner Peck describes to us—in an awareness of *amazing grace* about us. It becomes apparent to us that it is taking an almost inexhaustible store of grace just to get us through an ordinary life with some degree of purpose and dignity. And as we live, we become more and more aware of this outside help—of strength and mercy and aid that come to us.

Slowly, this grace begins to have a voice and a face and a presence. Grace laughs and cries with us until it is transformed into a person, and grace becomes Jesus to us. And as we come to know Him, more of the falseness and pretense of life fall away. The better we know Him, the more we become ourselves.

But there is another step in drawing near to life. *Grace has become Jesus* to us and, as we walk along with Him, *Jesus becomes all*. Suddenly, one is gripped with the realization that life is as Julian of Norwich said,

> Everything which he has made . . . is great, generous, and beautiful and good. But the reason why it seemed in my eyes so little was because I saw it in the presence of him who is the Creator. To any soul who sees the Creator of all things all that is created seems very small . . . everything which is beneath him is not sufficient for us.

It may only come to us in glimpses. We may not be able to bring our lives into total harmony with its richness. Still, we know it to be true, for grace has become Jesus, and Jesus has become all.

I was up in a retreat in Illinois a couple of years ago and they were following their custom of joke-telling during the meals. The microphone was left on and anyone who wished to do so could tell the rest of us a joke. Most of those would-be comedians should hold on to their day jobs.

During lunch one day a kid of about sixteen delivered a one-liner that at least got my attention. He said, "A hypocrite is a man in church holding his wife's hand while singing 'All That Thrills My Soul Is Jesus.'" I like to sing that song and, if we are in church together, I am probably holding Peg's hand. That is why it is good for me to sing another song, too: "I dare not trust the sweetest frame . . ." because when I am singing those words, I am not thinking about my motorcycle. I am thinking of a little five-foot lady who has been my wife for thirty years. And I need to keep on singing: ". . . but wholly lean on Jesus' name." For it is really only as He becomes all to me that I can be all I should be to her, and she be all she can be to me. The closer we can live to Him, the more alive and real we become. For He is the Life of life. This becomes easier for me to see when I try to think of Him as the life of my days.

Last Christmas was one of the brightest, happiest times I can remember. My heart is still filled with such delightful memories that I am smiling just thinking about it.

We had just moved into a new house. Well, it was new to us anyway. After twenty years in your other place, you wonder whether you will ever be able to feel you are at home in the new one.

Our old house had grown with the family over the years. Robert and Mike and I had remodeled the garage into a recreation room. Later, with the help of a real carpenter, we had added a dining room, primarily to display some stained-glass windows we found in a junk shop. The kitchen had been enlarged and a sunny plant room attached. Finally, a guest house with a place for a study for me was added, until we sprawled across the hillside overlooking Old Hickory Lake. Now we had decided to move closer to town. We wondered, though, if we could ever find a place we would learn to love as well as our lakeside home.

When we drove by and saw the "For Sale" sign in the yard, we knew this faded brown New England saltbox with the yellow door was for us. With some paint and wallpaper, it has become an almost perfect setting for Peg's antiques and primitives.

This was really our second move within the year. It seems like we've been moving to Birmingham twenty miles at a time. Rather, it was Peg's second move. I was in the hospital when the time came to leave the other house. So Peg and the kids moved. But when I got out, I found them. She can't get away from me. I've told her if she ever decides to leave me to pack my bags too, because I am going with her.

The people from the church had helped pack, move, and put everything away again in the condominium where we were going to live until we could decide where to settle more permanently. At least they helped her put away all you could squeeze into a three-bedroom condominium from eleven rooms and a guest house. We had a lot of stuff stored in our friends' attics and basements all over town. One of the reasons it was so good to get in the new house was to unpack things that we hadn't seen in months. It was like a housewarming shower all over again.

One of the things that we unpacked was the manger scene. The figures are wooden carvings and they are complete even down to two, tiny sleeping roosters. On vacations over the years, I have collected stones and bits of driftwood from hikes and woods and walks on beaches to make the stall and the manger and the background. So setting up the crèche is my job. When I first started, Peg thought it would be better if I did it in the playroom. But I have gotten so good at it that this year she let me put it in the living room on her new wicker coffee table top. It was one of my better efforts, if I say so myself. And it seemed to speak to all of us anytime we went into the living room. A couple of nights we sat in front of the manger and listened to "The Messiah." Once in awhile I think we ought to set it up in June.

And all of the children were going to be here in our new home. Nothing can make a father of five any happier than to have them all home at once. Especially with the bonus of daughters-in-law and a grandson. Leigh had gotten home early in December. She had been there to help pick out the tree and to help her mother decorate the house and hang the wreaths on the doors. Tom and Patrick had given up their rooms to their older married brothers and moved in on Leigh's sofa.

For once I had done my shopping early, but on Christmas Eve morning, Leigh and I made one last desperate trip just for old times' sake. When we got home at noon, the aroma of the turkey baking in the oven wafted through the house. I puttered around the house but I was really keeping an eye on the driveway for the maroon VW convertible that was bringing Mike and Gwen home to us from Kansas City, where he is in his graduate seminary program. The school where Gwen teaches music didn't get out until the afternoon of the twenty-third, and they were driving halfway that night and the rest of the way on Christmas Eve.

Late in the afternoon Robert and Jetta were going to fly in from Chicago. He was planning to leave his marketing agency office a little early in time to pick Jetta up at the hospital where she is a medical technician. And they would catch the plane that would bring them home to us.

After dinner we were all going to an eleven o'clock Christmas Eve candlelight service. The pastor and his family were out of town and I had been asked to be in charge. Mike was going to read the Scripture and some of my favorite friends were singing. All of my family would be seated in the first pew, and I knew I would be having the happy privilege of seeing their faces bathed in brightness as they each lit a Christmas candle.

Need I tell you that my heart was so full of happy anticipation and mingled memories that my feet were barely touching the floor?

Then, as if I didn't have enough to be happy about, a few days before, I had received some fine news from the surgeon. No surgery in January. You don't know what this means to a coward. I had been too sick during the surgery back in the spring for them to complete what they had started out to do. Now he told me that a procedure was being perfected that might enable them to correct what they had begun. Not only was the surgery not going to be completed in January, but I could wait, and then maybe, the whole procedure could be reversed.

So as Christmas came to our house, I felt most wonderfully blest. Good health, good news, a large, loving family, a new home and lots of friends to share it.

But it was not Christmas because we had a new house. It was Christmas because Jesus brings us life. Not everybody had a new home. A young couple in our church, Rick and Jeanie, came home a few days before Christmas to find their apartment in flames and everything they owned—gone.

It was not Christmas because all of the kids were home. It was Christmas because Jesus has come. Not everybody had their loved ones with them. The only sad part about Christmas this year was that Mom and Dad were far away in Florida where he was recuperating from a painful illness. It was the first time in years we had not all gone over to their house for Christmas morning breakfast, including freshly-squeezed orange juice and homemade biscuits.

And it was not Christmas because I had good news from the doctor. It was Christmas because Jesus was born. Not everybody had good news from the doctor. Back in the summer when I was in the hospital for a short second trip, a friend of ours was also admitted. She was on the floor above me. In the spring she had received the same grim diagnosis the doctor had given me. We knew the whole family well. When I directed the Fourth Generation, a teen group in our church, her kids, Ronnie and Becky, were in it. I learned to love them both. I had gone to school with her husband, Paul. She was buried a few days before Christmas.

Still, it was Christmas at the Langfords'; it was Christmas at the folks' in Fort Myers; it was Christmas at the Shields'. It was Christmas because *Jesus is born*. There is no Christmas without Him. And all the rest is just tinsel on the tree.

And Christmas is the time to sing those eloquent, life-giving words—"Jesus is born, Jesus is born."

> Just as those words came and changed a barn filled with cows and straw into a shrine, a hillside dotted with sheep and shepherds into a cathedral, a sky filled with stars into a message from the Father—so they come to you:
>
> as old as eternity—
> as fresh as the morning—
> as simple as a baby—
> as majestic as a psalm—
> Warm as a mother's arms—
> Mighty as God Himself—
> Jesus is born.
>
> All of the celebrations of our Christmases begin at a manger with Him.
>
> We say, Merry Christmas, because He is our joy and our happiness.
>
> We say, Goodwill to men, because He is our peace and our pardon.
>
> We say, Good tidings of great joy, because He is our announcement and proclamation.
>
> We say, Good cheer, because He is our hope and our confidence.
>
> We say, Emmanuel, because He is with us.
>
> We sing, Glory to God, because His light blesses us.
>
> The light shined in the darkness and it still shines, and shines, and shines. And when our lights flicker and die—when those with whom we have long celebrated are gone—when we can no longer share needs or ex-

> change gifts or sing songs—it will still be Christmas because Jesus is Born, Jesus is Born.

And the same is true with all of the rituals and all the events of our lives: Thanksgivings, birthdays, commencements, funerals, weddings and all the others are tied just as inexorably to Him. He is the very center of all the days of our lives. These words Jesus uses in John 15:5 are pointed, but they are true: "Apart from me . . . nothing."

He is not saying that He is the life of the Christian, although that is true. He is not saying that he is the life of the church, although He is. He is saying that He is the *Life of life*.

Chewing Gum Wrappers

Jesus came to do the work of the Father.

His life was lived between "I must be about My Father's business" and "I have finished the work You gave Me to do." He lived in preparation for, dedication to, and performance of the will of the Father.

It came so easily to Him. It was almost as much a part of Him as breathing. Remember the Sabbath morning at the Sheep Pool? They called it Bethesda and it meant House of Mercy.

The story of the Sheep Pool itself was based on an ancient superstition. So strongly was the feeling that it was folklore that some translations omit altogether the parts about the troubling of the water and the gift of healing for the first person to immerse himself in the swirling pool.

It might have been a deep pool above some subterranean stream that bubbled up periodically. But the belief was that the waters were disturbed by an angel, and the first person to plunge into them would be cured.

No one seems to know where this old, old story got started. There was no record of how often the waters were troubled or how many had been healed across the years if, indeed, anyone had. It was not really much of a hope—but it was a hope—and sometimes hopes are hard to come by.

And so that morning among the colonnades there was a great crowd of sick people—the blind, the lame, and the paralyzed. They were children of their age. Maybe this would be the day when the waters would surge and one of them would be close enough and fast enough to be the first into the pool. And he or she would go home cured.

There is something different about cities on the Sabbath. It is not like the days of commerce and work. The streets are quiet. Few people are moving about. The shops and stalls are closed.

It was a quiet day for Jesus as well. There is no mention of either the disciples or a crowd being with Him. Walking along alone in the early morning, He turned down a side street. It was almost as if the light had changed or He had crossed the street to walk in the sunshine.

His eyes fall upon a man lying against one of the five colonnades—a man who had been crippled for thirty-eight years. One can only imagine a bit about this cripple and how he had made his way again today to this place.

"Do you want to be cured?" Jesus asks him.

"There is no one to put me in the pool when the waters are troubled," the man replies.

"Then why don't you get up and go home?"

And he arose and was well.

And Jesus went on with His walk.

It was later in the day before the story was finally put together by the Jews. And they asked Jesus why He would do this kind of work on the Sabbath. His answer was as disarming as it was maddening to them.

"My Father was working—and I was just helping."

Jesus saw His Father at work that morning in that place of misery and misplaced hopes. The sick and the paralyzed with their pain and agony make us wonder where the Father has gone and why He is not doing something about it. Jesus saw them and saw His Father among them at work—and He joined Him. Naturally, effortlessly, comfortably, He did the work of the Father. It not only seemed natural to Him, *it seemed to be the delight of His life.*

Again, in His early ministry, we find Jesus by Jacob's well, close by the village of Sychar in Samaria. The disciples had left Him there while they went into the village to buy something for lunch.

Jesus is sitting in the shade of the trees by the well as a woman comes alone with her waterpot to draw water at noonday. Her face, her countenance, her eyes, the stoop of her shoulders tell her story to Jesus. And Jesus tells her a story—a story of living water—water that would quench her thirst and would again put life in the spirit her tired, defeated eyes reveal.

She was just beginning to believe when the disciples came back. Maybe it was that she was embarrassed. They looked so astonished when they saw Jesus talking to her. Or maybe she was ashamed because they ignored her completely. Anyway, she left her waterpot and went back into the village to tell anyone who would listen, of her conversation with the man at the well.

The disciples spread the lunch and told Jesus it was time to eat. But He tells them He has already eaten. They look around for a McDonald's bag or some evidence of some lunch. Not that I think He would throw trash on the ground.

"Maybe somebody else brought Him some food," they wonder.

And He explains, "I had lunch with my Father."

We call it work. He said it was meat and drink to Him.

In the church there always seems to be the need for devising some new plan with a catchy title and slogan to once again enroll the saints in the Father's work. It's even better if someone writes a song for the kickoff rally. It is usually about as easy to sing as "The Star-Spangled Banner."

Once in our fellowship we had a denomination-wide program to help us find those in the community who needed Christ. We were all trained. Leaders came from headquarters to teach us in district gatherings and then in zone meetings and finally in each local church. We were armed with the forms and cards and door-opening questions.

"Do you know a boy or girl in this neighborhood who does not go to Sunday school?"

We call it Visitation Evangelism, but He calls it lunch. We sometimes call it Thursday Night Visitation, but He calls it dinner. We may call it Soul-winning, but He says it is fried chicken and green beans and sliced tomatoes and a tall glass of iced tea. Jesus came to do the work of the Father and He liked it as well as He did eating.

Wouldn't it be nice to start out to witness with the kind of anticipation we have when we are going to dinner, rather than feeling like we feel when we are going out to witness? Did you ever go to anyone's house for supper and knock on the door, hoping they weren't home—like you do when you are calling for the church? Would we need to have a witness night at all if we were always seeing the Father at work and it was just like pulling up to the table to help Him?

Jesus is telling us here about a relationship that could make this true in our lives. He is saying, "My Father is the Gardener. I am the Vine. You are the branches."

And the branches that live in the Vine will be cultivated and tended by the Gardener and they will be nourished and supported by the Vine and they will bear much fruit.

Two of the things I believe are always present in the words of Christ are *high privilege* and *deep responsibility*. And I think they are both here, too.

There is a very satisfying privilege to those of us He is calling branches. What He is really saying presents itself to me in a way that is so simple that I don't know why I often overlooked it.

If I were part of a tree, I don't think I'd want to be the trunk. In the first place, a great part of the trunk is buried in the dirt and mud. The bigger the tree, the more there is way down there where it is dark and dirty. Always, it has to keep spreading out down in the earth in search of moisture and nourishment. And then the branches are not usually very thoughtful, and they reach out in every direction as far as they can and they love to swing in the wind. And the more fun they have, the bigger the problems of weight and balance for the poor old trunk. Then there are the obvious hazards of sign hangers with hammers, and romantics with knives, not to mention woodpeckers and lumberjacks.

I think I'd rather be a branch. In the spring, branches burst into delicate buds. They furnish shade for summer picnics. They are ladders for little boys to climb to the skies. Branches blossom and flower to tell us all that there will be more trees. And branches bear fruit—like big, juicy red apples that you can shine on your sleeve and bite into while the juices dribble down your chin. I'd rather be a branch than a trunk.

And Jesus is saying to us all that He will be the trunk and we can be the branches. Can you hear Him saying to you that He will bear you up—in the summer's sun, in winter's storm—He will nourish and water you—that you will only be barren for a season—that you will soon burst forth in leafy foliage, in radiant blossom, and in life-giving fruit? He is saying something very good to us when He says, "My Father is the Gardener, I am the Trunk and you are the branches."

I know I am an inveterate *privilege-looker*, but one can hardly fail to see there is also a lot of responsibility here as well. It seems that it goes without saying, but just let me remind you of some things of which His words remind me.

One is that gardeners do not bear fruit. You never saw a gardener with tomatoes hanging down from his arms, did you? Gardeners select the field and prepare the soil and plant the seed and chop the weeds and prune the plants. But they don't bear fruit.

And trunks don't bear fruit. They support the weight, and seek out the moisture. They hold the branches up to the sunlight. They bear branches but they don't bear fruit.

Branches bear fruit—and we are the branches. Suddenly, He seems to be saying to us that if there is any fruit borne in the places where we are, we will be the bearers. And if we are not fruitful, there won't be any fruit at all. At least, not until He grows some new branches.

In this simple way He is telling us that we are to be doing what branches are supposed to do. He is talking about our purpose and our place in life.

If you have the feeling that you are the one who is

supposed to keep the saints free of weeds—lay down the hoe. That is the gardener's job. The Father is the Gardener. If it seems to you the weight of the whole church is resting on you—set it down. The trunk will take care of that, and Jesus is the Trunk. You are a branch and branches bear fruit—much fruit—fruit that will last.

Sometimes it is hard to remember, if indeed we ever really knew, why we are. Most of us could be filed under *Miscellaneous*.

I think of a car I happened to be driving behind in a recent election year in our state. We had a gubernatorial candidate whose name was Jake Butcher. It is not easy to build a campaign slogan around the name "Jake Butcher." It sounds like an announcement for a meat-cutters' convention. The slogan was "Jake in '78" which, incidentally, turned out to be erroneous. On the left side of the bumper was this campaign message, "Jake in '78." In the middle of the bumper was a sticker that read, "Jesus is Lord." And on the right side was this startling revelation: "Sailors have more fun." It made one wonder who was driving the car and where on earth he was going!

It isn't that most of us don't have any direction at all. Usually, we have so many directions in which we are trying to go that no one is the least bit surprised that we aren't sure, either. I felt a little more comfortable with the car whose bumper sticker stated honestly, "Don't Follow Me—I'm Lost."

These phrases that He is using tell us why we are here. He is describing the relationship as one that issues forth in a fruitful life.

I have been using the phrase, "bear fruit," like we both understood it to mean the same thing. Maybe we should come to an understanding about that.

In its strictest sense I believe we all think first of the

Great Commission. We are to go, to bear witness, to baptize, and to teach. Ultimately the things we do are done *to make disciples.* We understand that the task is to *win souls.* Still, it appears to me that even though this was the ultimate or strictest good for Jesus, He went about it in the broadest way possible.

I once saw a sign on the front of a church that announced:

Our Soul Goal For September is 200

The phrase *soul goal* makes me think of something like scalps or notches on a gun. It does not adequately describe what I believe Jesus was trying to accomplish through us. Jesus was always aware that souls are packaged in bodies, and they are people. People get cold and hungry and thirsty and lonely. Sometimes they get sick and sometimes they are thrown into prison. And He tells us that they are very important to Him—so important that whatever is done or left undone in their behalf was just the same as doing or not doing for Him. His life is interwoven with people.

So closely does He identify himself with people everywhere that he tells his disciples: "When they are hungry, I am hungry; when they are cold, I am cold; when they are lonely, I am lonely. Whoever they are and wherever you find them, remember that when they bleed, I bleed; when they cry, I cry; when they are thrown into prison, I am thrown into prison. And whatever you do for them, you are doing for me. And whenever you pass them by, you are passing me by."

All these things He is describing, then, are the work of the kingdom. They are parts of the processes of God that lead to His redemptive purposes. Anything, then, even down to a cup of cold water poured in His name, is properly the work of the branches, and branches bear fruit.

So the working definition of "bearing fruit" for me has become "anything which helps anybody into any knowledge of God."

There are three essential characteristics of such a deed—it touches somebody, it is done in love, and it is done in His name. Therefore, the simplest of deeds done by the least likely of us in the humblest of circumstances becomes fruit of the kingdom. And when He said, "branches bear fruit," He was making a promise—it can be so in your life.

I want to make some simple suggestions about "cups of cold water." The first of them is *hugs*.

For a number of years Peg and I were teachers in the Sunday school. I taught the college class and she taught in the nursery. At the present we are going to class together. I think my "ministry" of "fruit-bearing" still has to find its expression in some way around the church. My unofficial post is across the hallway just outside the classroom door. We go to early service and then to Sunday school class. After class the hall is filled with people. Those of us who come to the first service are happy because we are ready to go to lunch now. The rest of the people, who are going from class to the sanctuary for the eleven o'clock service, are also happy because it is always good to be in our worship service.

Now let me tell you that I am, or at least have always wanted to be, a lover. I have never had any disposition at all to be a fighter. A couple of years ago we were at the class Christmas party at the home of one of the three teachers. I was standing with Wilson, one of my friends, near the front door. The host and hostess were busy elsewhere in the house and, if they didn't hear the doorbell, Wilson and I let the guests in and showed them where to put their coats and how to get to the punch bowl. After a while, he said to me:

"Why is it that everybody who comes in shakes my hand and hugs your neck?"

"Well, the reason is simple. When people come in, you hold out your hand. They might want to hug you, but they can't get to you with that big old hand sticking out there. If you would just open your arms, they would walk right into them."

And sure enough, after about four more arrivals, he saw my point.

So I was standing at my post in the hall one Sunday after class, ready to serve, when a little old lady whom I have known for a long time came from her class toward me.

She lives alone now because her husband is dead, and, like the rest of us, her children are too busy with their own children to come home much at all. So I opened my arms and she walked right into them. I closed them about her and told her that I loved her. I asked her how she was and she told me. And she went on to church.

Someone told me later that she had heard I had been hugging ladies at church again. When I asked her how she knew, she said, "Birchie came into the sanctuary yesterday morning and sat down beside me. With tears in her eyes, she told me that you had put your arms around her and told her you loved her."

Sometimes it is easy to recruit people for this ministry. I was talking about this one evening on a college campus. The next morning was High School Senior Day when kids from all over come to take a look at the school. As I came to chapel that morning, it warmed my heart to see a couple of upperclassmen already putting this good truth into practice. A college could have worse advertising.

At other times, it is a bit more difficult. Every once in a while I go to church where the pastor says to me, "I sure hope you are not one of those dudes that has us all holding hands." I hate to tell him. Sometimes, when I ask people to join hands, I tell them that Peg and I squeeze each other's hands and that means "I love you." And I ask them to squeeze hands. Not everybody gets *squuz*. It takes all the courage some people have to join hands—much less squeeze. I always tell everybody that didn't get *squuz* to see me after church.

And if that is true about joining hands, you can imagine the consternation of a general call to embracing.

I'm afraid you will think I am just a sentimental, weepy-eyed, soft-hearted fool. Well, I am, but what I am saying to you is very, very true. I want to quote an authority or two so you won't throw this theory out the window without any serious consideration.

In Sidney B. Simon's book, *Caring, Feeling, Touching,* he writes that we all have "a deep-seated hunger within us that no amount of food can satisfy." It is a "hunger for the touch, the feel, the concrete reality of human contact. Quite literally, it is 'skin hunger.'" And he says that it is not hard to tell the difference between young people who have grown up with their need to be held and love satisfied and those who have rarely been touched. Those who have been treated with openness and warmth "tend to be open, warm, and relaxed." Those who have not "often seem to be more withdrawn . . . even hostile. You can see them on any playground shoving, wrestling, fighting. Inside the schools they push each other down the stairs, shove faces into the drinking fountain, throw food in the lunchroom. And behind every shove . . . is an unheard cry of skin hunger."

As a professor, Mr. Simon tries to teach touching to students, to family, to friends. He, too, runs into some difficulty. He describes the "A-Frame Hug" where two people touch heads and lean into each other like a ski lodge. Sometimes he says, people get so nervous they start patting each other on the back as if they were burping a baby. Still, he concludes, "Touching and being touched makes better people."

My son Mike is a hugger, too. He's preparing for the ministry and he'll make a good one, because he opens himself up to people like a big teddy bear. When Mike first met his girlfriend's father, he was a little nervous. After a time or two, though, Mike just reached out and grabbed Bert like Bert wanted him in the family. I think Bert was afraid of Mike for a while then.

I think I know, having a daughter myself, a little of what that father was thinking when his daughter brought a boy from Tennessee to Colorado for Easter break. Mike just never would let him get far enough away from him to dislike him. They are good friends now. When they meet, you can't tell who grabs whom first. Bert is a good father-in-law. I believe he is as proud of his son-in-law, Mike, as I am of my daughter-in-law, Gwen.

It would seem that there is hardly a more likely place for one to begin in the world than in the area of loneliness and hurt. Jane Howard, in her book entitled *Families*, has a list of ten earmarks of a good family. One of these is that a good family is affectionate. "More and more," she writes, "I realize that everybody, regardless of age, needs to be hugged and comforted in a brotherly or sisterly way now and then. Preferably *now*."

Now let me tell you a story about *prayers*. Hugs, and now prayers. It, too, took place in the same hall outside the classroom where I usually "minister." This day a lady came up to me and asked me if I knew who she was. It took me a moment but as soon as she told me, I remembered. She then related this story to me:

"A few weeks ago, I was impressed to pray for you

in a special way. Your face and your name were before me. And I did pray as I was directed. I started to write you a note and mention it to you, but I thought you might think I was crazy or something, so I didn't. After a while I dropped you from the list. Later, I had the same thought about you and prayed again. So when I saw you this morning, I thought I would tell you about it."

I thanked her and we visited a bit and she went on down the hall to the sanctuary.

Neither of us really had any idea why she had been led to pray for me. There didn't seem to be any special need. A few months later I came home for a week or so before going out to Oklahoma to speak. I was not feeling very well. After a few days I went to see the doctor and he sent me across the street to the hospital. It was the beginning of a period of serious illness, emergency surgery, and slow recovery. It was eight weeks before I would finally go home again.

I do not really understand all about this. What had happened was a conversation between God and my friend that went something like this:

"Pat, I want you to be praying about Bob Benson."

Well, all right, God, let me tell you about Bob Benson.

My first thought was, *Why should He tell her to tell Him about me?* Then it began to come to me that, while He was telling her to *tell Him about me,* He was also telling her to *tell me about Him.* And some two months before the reason was apparent to either of us, Pat was praying for me.

This past winter I was asked to speak in the devotional services at the Benson Choir Directors' Clinic. One morning I was standing in the lobby before the morning worship time. The people were having coffee and doughnuts and visiting with each other before going into the conference room. I was acting like some kind of gospel hero, listening to kind remarks and autographing books. I always tell them that if I sign them, they can't return them for credit. Seriously, right then I was thinking about the next half hour and needing a moment of quiet. Someone tapped me on the shoulder and I turned to look at a young woman, who said to me:

"Is there anything I can pray for you today?"

It was the nicest thing that was said to me that morning.

I am learning that there isn't anything you can do for people that helps more than praying. It is like S. D. Gordon writes, "You can do *more* than pray, *after* you pray. But you *cannot* do more than pray *until* you have prayed."

Let me add another to the list. It is *letter writing*. In this instance, as in prayer, its meaning is apparent to me because it happened *to me*.

In the hospital I received a steady stream of cards and letters from people everywhere. From Trevecca, where I had been serving as temporary college chaplain, I got a card twenty by forty inches. They set it in the lobby of the chapel building for several days and most of the students and faculty signed it.

Roxie Gibson, a close personal friend of Peg's and mine, is an elementary school teacher and she had her class make cards with pictures and Scripture verses. One little girl did a lovely card with tulips and trees and butterflies. For the verse inside, she had selected Romans 10:21:

"But to Israel He saith, 'All day long I have stretched forth my hands unto a disobedient and obstinate people.'"

Get well soon.

Your friend,
Stacey.

I sure hope she didn't know something I didn't.

The realization that so many people would open their hearts to me was a daily source of strength and help.

Just last week there was a letter from the wife of a pastor. She said that her husband had used something I had written in his message that evening. It was 1:30 in the morning when she wrote:

> So thank God He is using you even today on the mission field. You are a blessing and we care about you. If you are ill, I'm sorry. If you hurt, I care. We have prayed for you every day but felt compelled tonight to claim your healing. So out under the British sky with God's stars overlooking, we thanked God for your complete healing. God bless you today in a *special* way.

It was written by hand on an ordinary tablet—one of those with the blue lines. It took only twenty-six pence to mail. But it is not ordinary to me. And I find myself wanting to live and write in a way that again commits to paper words that could be used by a California pastor speaking in a conference in England.

A letter, a note, a card are simple effective ways for the branches of your life to overhang the fences of others anywhere.

So I have given three suggestions: *Hugs* and *prayers* and *letters*. Each of them is a way for you to reach out to someone else. Each requires a bit of action on your part. Just in case even that is more initiative than you are prepared to take, I want to mention one more thing. It is the ministry of *listening*.

Carl Rogers has been a central figure in the field of humanistic or person-centered psychology for more than three decades. His latest book, *A Way of Being*, describes how over the years he came to a person-centered approach to life. About "listening" he writes:

> When I truly hear a person . . . and when I let him know I heard his own private person meanings, many things happen. I have often noticed that the more deeply I hear the meanings of this person, the more there is that happens. Almost always, when a person realizes he has been deeply heard, his eyes moisten. I think in some real sense he is weeping for joy. It is as though he were saying, "Thank God, somebody heard me. Someone knows what it's like to be me."

He likens such moments to a prisoner in a dungeon tapping out a coded message day after day: "Does anybody hear me? Is anybody there?" Finally one day someone taps back, "Yes." And the word coming back releases him from his loneliness. There are lots of people today who are living in private prisons. Only if you listen will you hear the faint messages from within.

The amazing thing is that when one really learns to listen, much less talk is required. You do not have to have the answer if you can truly hear the questions. I am trying to learn to look at people and listen. I am trying to be *all there* as they speak. I am trying not to think of what I am going to say when they finish. I am trying to listen. Sometimes I have been able to do so and when I have, it helps.

Last week I was talking to a lady in a crowded room. To tell you the truth, it was hard to keep from glancing over her shoulder at whomever I might be talking to next. Later, she wrote me a note that made me realize it was a more important meeting than I knew.

> When I talked to you yesterday—you looked at me—*in my eyes* like you really wanted to hear me—that somehow you knew I was hurting—though we didn't talk about it. I wanted you to know you ministered to me and I needed it. Sometimes people think if you're in the ministry, you don't need ministering to!

Hugs, prayers, letters, listening. These are ordinary ways of living. But if it touches somebody, if it is done in love, and if it is done in His name, it is fruit of the Kingdom.

A simple thing happened to us recently which more than ever made me believe this. I was sitting in the bedroom reading when Peg came in and exclaimed, "This is why we go to that church!" I looked up and she was holding a chewing gum wrapper. And she read to me:

> Dear Patrick, (that's our youngest)
> God loves you—
> and so do I.
>
> Uncle Pek

Pek Gunn is not really our uncle. But his own son died in infancy and so he decided if he was not anyone's father, he would be everybody's uncle. Then, too, he didn't have too much choice because Frances, his wife, had already decided to be everybody's aunt. She taught a Sunday school class in the children's department. She taught me and she taught Peggy. Later, she taught each of our children. She died awhile back, so she won't teach our grandson. Uncle Pek and Aunt Frances and chewing gum wrappers.

Peg laid the wrapper on the chest a day or so later, and Patrick saw it and said, "Hey, that's my chewing gum wrapper." And he took it back to his room to put it among his "special" things.

Yes, I guess that's a pretty good indication of why we go to that church. If I make it—and surely I'm closer to the end than I am to the beginning—it will be because my parents got me in with the right crowd.

> When I raced ahead,
> they watched and prayed
> and came along behind.

When I was down,
  they picked me up
    and dusted me off.
When I fell behind,
  they slowed down
    and waited till I caught up.
They comfort me when I cry,
  come to see me when I'm sick,
Pray with my kids at the altar
  when I am away
    praying with someone else's.
They write notes on gum wrappers
  and build walls of love
    around us all.

Do you wish you were in a crowd like that? It only takes one to start—someone who hugs, someone who prays, someone who writes notes, someone who listens. Start a crowd where you are. It can be at home. It can be at church. It can be at work. It can be anywhere.

And Jesus was telling us:
  My Father is the Gardener,
    I am the Trunk—
      you are the branches
    and branches bear fruit.

Downward Mobility

I had been president of the company for just a few months when I saw a book advertised by the American Management Association. The title reminded me of one of my *strongest weaknesses.* The book was written by Joseph Batten and was entitled *Tough-Minded Management.* Since I was not nearly as tough as I should have been, I immediately sent for the book. When it arrived and I unwrapped it, I was pleased. The title emblazoned on the dust jacket was stated three times in big, bold type:

Tough-Minded Management
Tough-Minded Management
Tough-Minded Management

Besides, this was the third edition and surely by now Mr. Batten was tougher than ever. Maybe by the time I finished reading and underlining, I would become a triple-tough president. And that would surely make me closer to what the company needed in the times in which we were operating.

I guess I expected too much from just one book. It was very fine and shouldn't be judged solely on its effect or lack of the same on me. Mr. Batten very lucidly explained and elaborated a basic style and philosophy of management in which I believed, and so I thought he was a very smart man. People with whom I agree seem remarkably intelligent to me. Underlying all of the management information in the book was a powerful indication of his insight into people and, moreover, into life itself. But the statement that gripped me the most from the entire book was this: "Over the long pull it is impossible to give away more than you can receive."

It seemed an unlikely place for this statement to appear. It certainly was not an expression I expected to see in regard to *toughness in management*. But there it was. And it is also here in the fifteenth chapter of John. Jesus is saying, "A man *should lay down* his life."

It is a radical idea to most of us that the results of our living will not be measured in terms of what we have been able to accumulate or acquire or hold tightly to. Even more startling to contemplate is that such results are important, rather, in relation to how well we have been able to let go of, to release, to *lay down* our lives. The society in which we live places most of its emphasis on picking up.

I think we are accustomed to phrases that Frederick Beuchner describes as the

> kind of worldly wisdom that more or less all men have been living by since the cave man:
>
> You've got your own life to lead.
> Business is business.
> Charity begins at home.

Don't get involved.
God helps those who help themselves.
Safety first.
Drive carefully—the life you save may be your own.

Hagar sums it up for us very well in the funny papers when he gives two rules for happiness:

1. Be content with what you've got.
2. Be sure you've got plenty.

For instance, at least once a year as a principal owner of the company, I was asked by the banks to submit a personal financial statement. It had a place in the left-hand column for a listing of all my assets: cash on hand, U.S. Government securities, accounts and loans receivable, notes receivable, life insurance cash surrender value, stocks and securities, real estate, automobiles, and other assets (marked *itemize*). On the other side was a place for a listing of all my liabilities. I always needed more room for this side. There were places to list notes to banks secured and unsecured, loans against life insurance, accounts payable, taxes payable, mortgages against real estate, and any other liabilities (also marked *itemize*). At the bottom of the sheet there was a place to combine those two lines, the total assets and the total liabilities. The difference between those two numbers was called my *net worth*.

That number largely indicated to the bank the kind of customer I was and how I was to be treated. The larger the net worth, the more important I was to the bank. It dictated the title of the officer with whom I dealt and into which executive dining room I was occasionally invited for lunch. Generally, it seems to be true in banking that if you can prove you don't need any money, it will be very easy for you to borrow some. If you can prove that you do not need any at all, they will probably let you have as much as you want. It is only when you need it that they are a little sticky.

We all know about the process of trying to make sure that line seventeen is larger than line thirty-one, so that line thirty-three represents enough *net worth* to keep us afloat in the world in which we find ourselves. But deep inside, most of us have a faint suspicion that what Jesus is telling us just might be true. And we live wondering what is *real* net worth.

The reconciliation of these two counter-claims on us is probably among the most difficult issues that we face in our quest for the shared life. Somewhere between selling all we have and giving it to the poor and obligating ourselves for far more than we need or use or can pay for, lies the gate to faith and freedom. No relationship seems harder to define or to maintain than our relationship to our talents, strengths, weaknesses, accumulations, possessions, and energies.

And it is here that Jesus has something to tell us both with His words ("a man should lay down his life") and His own way of living. Two questions present themselves immediately.

This life style or ethic which Jesus describes is like a road bounded on either side by a ditch. The ditches are *ownership* and *accumulation*. One is *deep*, but the other is *deeper*. The latter is almost bottomless in its subtlety. Jesus walked serenely and confidently down the road. It is quite evident that He had resolved both of these issues that beset us all.

Jesus' prayer in the seventeenth chapter of John can be looked upon as a statement of His *real net worth*. In a sense, it is His line thirty-three. I don't think He could have borrowed very much money against it. But it was what He owned. It was what He had accumulated. And now He is telling the Father. A few words in one of the phrases tell us those things we need to know about how He avoided the ditches:

> *Father, protect by the power of Your name these men You have given me.*

For Jesus, line thirty-three was *these men*. They were the sum total of His years of ministry. In nearly every sense of the word they were His. He found them, loved them, called them, taught them, led them. No one could deny that He deserved them. But He does not claim that they are His. He does not pray *My men*. Rather, He says to the Father, "these men *You gave me*." Jesus had long before resolved the issue of *ownership*.

Once the ultimate question of ownership is established, maybe our other attitudes and relationships can begin to come into proper perspective and priority. Underneath any commitment to give part of ourselves away there will be the awareness that we are releasing something that was not ours to begin with—it has been given to us. We do not have what we have and we are not what we are by the quickness of our minds and the strength of our arms—although it may have taken a liberal application of both to be where we are today.

Who made your mind quicker than those about you? Who made your arm stronger? Certainly some explanation can be found in your willingness always to do more than was required of you. Your dogged determination not to quit until you had completed more than those who were competing against you is part of the answer, too. But where did you get that will to exceed? Did you just sit down one day and decide that you would have more discipline and willpower and skill than anyone else? No. It was in you; it was there; it was a gift; it had come to you.

I do not want to make light of your blood, sweat, and tears, but others have also bled, sweat, and cried, perhaps in deeper measure than you. And it has come back to them as nothing. Your successes, your accomplishments, your ability to pile up *net worth* were given to you. And when you lay them down, you will not be giving away things that you skillfully put together; you will be releasing something that came to you.

The legal form for an auto title has a couple of lines marked *lein holder*. If you paid cash for your car, of course, there is nothing indicated on either of those lines. If, on the other hand, the money needed for the purchase was loaned to you, someone or some institution will want it indicated that they, too, have part of the rights of ownership. They hold a *lein* against the vehicle. If you buy a home, the term is *mortgage* but it means the same. This is the legal recognition that the thing described does not belong solely to you.

And the question of *ownership* in life will not finally be resolved for any of us until we realize that we do not hold a clear title to anything. God has a prior claim. He is a lein holder. He has the mortgage. He furnished us with the wherewithal which we used in acquisition.

And this is not always an easy admission for us to make. Probably some of the very first words we all learned were *me* and *mine*. And it wasn't long afterward that we had to learn one more word, because people didn't listen to us when we said the first two. The third word was *no*.

I hadn't been in business long before I learned a basic truth. Unfortunately, it was as true about me as it was about everyone else. It had to do with signing agreements or contracts with people. The lesson was quite simple: Divide the profits before there are any. Try to make sure it is understood by everyone what is to be their share of the gains. Generally, everyone is fair and equitable over money that hasn't been made yet. But we all have a difficult time when we sit down to divide the money when it is lying on the table.

Then we begin to hear others say and, ruefully, to say ourselves:

> "Well, it was *my* idea . . ."
> "If it hadn't been for *me* . . ."
> "I worked longer than you did . . ."
> "I furnished the car . . ."
> "We started with *my* money . . ."

We may say any one of a dozen things but they all have a common meaning. They are said to establish our *claims of ownership* and they are said to minimize the rights of the other person.

One part of ownership is prudence. And one part of prudence is possessiveness. And one part of possessiveness is selfishness. And one part of selfishness is greed. And our claims to ownership find their basis somewhere in there between prudence and greed. it sounds better to call them prudent. Probably to the bystander, though, most of our prudence is hard to distinguish from greed.

We have a little dog whose name is Lady. There are times when Woman would have been a better name. She was sold to us as a French poodle but I have never seen the papers. At any rate, I don't think she is from downtown Paris. She thinks she's a hunting dog. Out where we used to live, she loved to chase squirrels and swim the lake and catch fish. At the new place she chases the horses in the adjoining pasture. One of these days she's going to catch one and then she is going to be in real trouble.

We feed her, of all things, dog food. When our family is going to be away for a few days, we take Lady over to Peg's folks to stay. Now Peg's mother is a real dog lover. She will scramble eggs for Lady's breakfast and fry her a hamburger patty or two for lunch. At dinner she shares her roast beef or chicken with her. She treats Lady royally. When Lady comes home after such elegant dining, she is not excited about the dog food at all. In fact, she refuses to eat it.

Our neighbors have a dog they found at a service station. They felt sorry for him and brought him home to keep him from getting run over. He is not even from rural France. I think his father traveled for a living. They call him, appropriately enough, Exxon.

I learned that the best way to get Lady off her high horse and on to dog food again was to take it out on the porch and offer it to Exxon. You have never seen such looks on a lady's face as we see when she rushes out to greet poor old Exxon. No longer is it a question of whether she wants it or not. It's even deeper than *need*. It has become a matter of *ownership* and Lady is going to *own it* even if she has to eat it.

And one of the real problems in *ownership* is the matter of holding on to what we claim to own. The process of *gathering up* is at the heart of our free enterprise system and as such is respected. We call it hard work, diligence, and *Yankee ingenuity*. Sometimes, though, our true colors are better revealed in the attitudes and actions surrounding our *holding on*. What seemed like prudence in *possessing* really becomes greed in *protecting*.

There is a deep correlation suggested in these words Jesus prayed, "Father, *protect* these men *You gave Me*." A simple test that might help us to discern the difference in our motives between prudence and greed would be to measure our willingness to entrust what we have to the Father's watch care and protection.

The English word *protect* comes from a Latin word which means *to cover in front*. And we are saying something significant about ourselves in the things we cover, shield, guard, watch over, maintain, endorse, and support, because we think they are *ours*.

It's like the old story about the conversation between the farmer and the Lord.

If I had a million dollars I'd give it to You, Lord.

If I had a thousand acres, I'd turn them over to You, Lord.

"Well, how about a pig?"

Take it easy there, Lord. I've got a pig.

And most of us are like the farmer—we've *got* and it is our *gots* that *get* us. Jesus is trying to show us and tell us *where we got it*. So the words *lay down your life* are calling us to resolve the question of ownership.

I have used four words in describing the boundaries of ownership—*prudence*, *possessiveness*, *selfishness*, and *greed*. In my mind they are progressive—each one carrying a little more will or intent than the one proceeding it. You choose the one that best describes you. Whichever one you use is your description of your attitudes toward *what you have*. Just to make sure you know I think it is a serious matter, I did put *greed* in the list.

In his very powerful book, *Celebration of Discipline*, Richard Foster describes the bondage of ownership as revealed by three inner attitudes.

> If what we have we receive as a gift, and if what we have is to be cared for by God, and if what we have is available to others, then we will possess freedom from anxiety. *This is the inward reality of simplicity*. However, if what we have we believe we have gotten, and if what we have we believe we must hold onto, and if what we have is not available to others, then we will live in anxiety.

The ditch on the other side of the road seems to me even deeper, because it would have to be to hold as many of us as are in it. I'm going to call it *accumulation*.

Property of
David & Becky Warren

It is nearly bottomless because it describes *what we think we have to have.*

On the one side the danger lies in ownership which, when left unattended, will show itself as greed. It is *covert greed*—observable and apparent, noticeable and obvious. That, in itself, sometimes puts some rein on it.

The second peril is all the more treacherous because it is *acquiescent greed.* It is closet greed, involuntary, unintended, accidental.

One of the E. B. White essays that I like best is entitled "Good-bye to 48th Street." He and his wife were moving to a new home and he is describing his attempts to "persuade hundreds of inanimate objects to scatter and leave me alone."

> A home is like a reservoir equipped with a check valve: the valve permits influx but prevents outflow. Acquisition goes on night and day—smoothly, subtly, imperceptibly. . . . Goods and chattels seek a man out. . . . Under ordinary circumstances, the only stuff that leaves a home is paper trash and garbage; everything else stays on and digs in.

One day he found himself on a sofa with a chip of wood and an honorary hood he had worn in an academic procession. The wood had been slightly gnawed by a beaver and then sent to him by one of his readers. He remarked:

> What I really needed at the moment was the beaver himself, to eat the wood. I shall never wear the hood again, but I have too weak a character to throw it away, and I do not doubt that it will tag along with me to the end of my days, not keeping me either warm or happy but occupying a bit of my attic space.

Our attics or garages or basements are probably no different from his—stuffed to overflowing with things bought at one time or another because we thought we needed them. And probably the reason we don't need them now is because the manufacturers and advertisers of America have convinced us that we needed something else to replace all that stuff that we now have stored.

We live in a society whose chief business is creating needs for us. Its slogan is "Bigger and Better" and the name of its anthem is "Upward Mobility." Kirkpatrick Sale has written a book to protest the supposed virtue of *bigness*. In *Human Scale* he lists the following items as some of the indications of our preoccupation with bigness:

> In the U.S. there are eleven different sizes of olives. The smallest size is "*jumbo*."
>
> The U.S. manufactures the largest newspapers in the world. *The New York Times*, the largest of them all, for an average Sunday in November, *any* November, weighs about ten pounds. It takes 840 acres of Canadian trees to produce one average Sunday's edition, more than it would take to build 100 three-bedroom ranch houses. It also costs New York City ten cents a copy in Sanitation Department expenses just to pick up the littered copies on Monday morning.
>
> American advertising expresses its most important messages in superlatives about size: the biggest shopping and travel card . . . the nation's largest airline with the world's biggest fleet of widebodies . . . the most spacious rooms in Boston . . . Big Macs, Whoppers, Jumbo Cokes, Green Giant . . . king size, super-longs, extra-large . . .

Whatever it is that we need to do, somebody has thought of a better way for us to do it. The lot on which our new house sits is just about an acre. When the amount of space covered by the house, driveway, patio, and sidewalks is taken out, I don't know exactly how much is left. But whatever there is needs mowing. There is a variety of equipment to do this job available for purchase or rental. There is a machine that you push and, as you push it, the wheels turn. They are connected to a reel and, when they turn, the reel turns and cuts the grass. You supply the power. There is also a machine that you push along, but it has a motor which turns the blade which cuts the grass. You only supply the power to turn the wheels. And there is a machine that you walk along behind, and the motor turns the wheels and the blade that cuts the grass. All you have to power is yourself. Best of all, of course, there is a machine that not only has a motor to turn the wheels and the blades but a seat—and you can ride along. All the power you have to supply is for steering. And a part of our economy is built on convincing people like me that what I really need to do the job right is the machine that I can ride on. And the advertisers work very hard to convince me that it is worth the 700- to 1000-dollar difference in the machines that accomplish the task.

Then, too, if they can convince me that I need to ride while I mow, it will be much easier for the health spa, exercycle, jogging shoe, and running suit people to sell me the equipment I need to get some exercise. Not to mention the assorted medicines and tranquilizers I need to take to relieve the stress that I build up because of a lack of physical activity in my life.

And what is true about lawnmowers is true about everything we can think of from automobiles to dolls. A fearsome part of our economy over the years has been the automobile industry and its ability to persuade us to turn in our *old* car for a *new* one about every two years. And most of the time the sole reason for trading is a difference in the way the sheet metal has been crunched on the outside.

Always there is a new model, something with a

new feature that is given to us as the reason we should trade up.

And if we are ever to make any progress at climbing out of the ditch of Accumulation we will have to learn to distinguish between *real needs* and *created needs*. Maybe the more proper words would be *real needs* and *created wants*.

Today we have only to ask two questions about what we want. The first is, "How much are the payments?" The other is, "How long do we have to make them?" In our credit-oriented society someone usually has a ready answer to both. And when these two questions are answered satisfactorily, we are ready to sign. If we can fit it into our *financial budget,* we will take it home with us or have it delivered Monday afternoon.

It may be time to see if it fits into our *energy budget*. For if we are going to lay down our lives, then somehow and at some place we are going to have to gain control of them so there is some left to lay down.

"Well, it is only $200 a month." But at $20 per hour you have just pledged ten hours a month, or two and a half hours a week toward a *real need* or a *created want*—chrome wheels and all. If you make half that much, you have pledged twice as much of your time and energy. If you make much less than that these days, you probably have two jobs and can't enjoy whatever it is they can't deliver until Wednesday anyway. But we have overdrawn our energy budget.

In His sermon on the mountain Jesus talked about this needless waste of our energies and emotions. His words are timely enough to have come from this morning's newspaper and speak to us where we are—"Be not anxious." Most of us have long since obligated ourselves into anxiety.

But He also suggests that there is an *affection budget*. In the same place he reminds us of the folly of trying to serve two masters—God and mammon. This solution is remarkably simple and direct: Seek the kingdom first. The great commandment is to love God with all of our heart. But it seems our heart is divided into a hundred pieces and scattered into all the places where we are keeping treasures.

So Jesus is making a very radical statement here. When nearly every other voice and instinct is telling us to hold on, He is saying to let go. He is responding to our very radical need. For if our hearts do not lead us into Ownership's ditch, then it is very likely that Research and Development along with Advertising and Marketing will soon have us in the other. Either way we are robbed, willfully or unintentionally, of the life we need to be laying down.

We don't mean to be frowning
at the supper table—
we are just too tired to smile.
We don't mean to be "absent'
when our sons want
to throw football.
It's just that most of us are still at the office.
It isn't that we don't want
to join in the conversation
on the way to church—
But in our minds we are busy talking
to the people that we owe.
We really mean to lay down our lives
just like He said—
And we will, too—
if we can ever get our hands on them.

Should, Ought, and Must

Some people love rules. Generally, I suspect it is because they are the rule makers. Maybe it is because I never seemed to get to make the rules, but I like the word *should* better than the word *ought*. And I like *ought* better than *must*. Usually it is the rule makers who use *ought* and *must*. But I like *should* best.

The rule makers love to post the rules. On our famous trip, I saw a sign in a village in England that read:

> **Parking Restricted Between 1st April and 30th September Each Year to Two Consecutive Hours At Any One Time Between The Hours of 8:30 A.M. and 6:30 P.M. on Any Day.**

I was glad I was on a bus.

Then a couple of years ago I was speaking at a retreat at a conference ground in southern California. Out in front of the dining hall was a large paved area. It was guarded by a sign which read:

No Parking—Ever

I wanted to rent a car. Something within me wanted to see if there really wasn't some time—even if it was in the wee hours of the morning—when you could just park there a minute or two. But the sign said *ever*. Not now, not during the millenium, not during eternity, not during lunch, not *ever*.

Some of the young couples at that same retreat were going to stay up late and play Rook one night. Staying up most of the night doesn't have nearly the appeal for me it once did, but they were expecting to have a good time. I told them it could not be as much fun as it used to be because Rook used to be against our rules. So we had double fun—playing the game and breaking the rules at the same time.

So you can see why I am intrigued by this use of the word *should* in this great statement of Jesus, *"A man should lay down his life."*

He could have said *ought* and it would be a true statement. And He could have said *must* and of course it would have been true. And He could have said *will* and it would be just as true. Because we are all somewhere in the process of *laying down* our life.

Last year I stood in the early spring sunshine at the graveside service reading some Scripture, making a few remarks, and praying at the burial of my aunt, Maggie Mai. My Uncle Robert had asked me to lead in these brief moments of memorial. I am his namesake and I felt honored to be invited to share in this deep time in his life. He sat quietly weeping as we buried his wife of nearly sixty-four years. As long as I can remember him he has been a shy, dignified, self-contained man. That afternoon, in his ninety-first year, burdened with the sorrow that is common to us all, he looked so lonely and frail that my heart ached for him.

I have passed his name on to my son and he, in turn, has passed it on to his. So now there are four of us—Robert Green Bensons all. We vary in ages a span of nearly eighty-five years, but there are commonalities about us all. One, of course, is our name. Another is that is as true of one of us as it is of the other—each of us is *laying down* his life. Little by little we are each in the process.

Young Rob is just losing his baby teeth. You just get two sets, you know, and here he is at age seven losing part of the first ones already. And I am losing what most everybody loses at so-called middle age. I guess I am middle-aged but, to tell you the truth, I don't know many people who are 102. My uncle had on a hearing aid that afternoon to try to hear what I was reading. I had on bifocals to try to read what he was hearing.

But this does not seem to me to be the context in which Jesus is thinking when He said *a man should lay down his life*. He does not seem to me to be telling us that we *must* lay life down or even that we *ought* to lay it down. And He does not even seem to be suggesting here that indeed we *are* doing so. He is reminding us that we *should*.

I am beginning to believe about the Scriptures that He is always trying to say something good to me. Even when He is *commanding*, I think if I could understand what He meant, I would find it is always something weighted with possibilities, surrounded by joy, and rooted in peace for me—from Him.

And *should* is the way I hear Him speaking to me. *Ought* and *must* speak with tones of enforcement—this is what will happen if you *don't*. *Should* seems to suggest more what will come to me if I *do*. And His voice does not ever seem to come to me in some sort of veiled threat, "*If you don't . . .*" It always seems to be coming to me as a gracious, gentle invitation, *"If you do . . ."*

So I think He is saying something very rich to us when He says, *A man should lay down his life.* I am beginning to get glimpses of this richness in different ways.

One of the things I hear Him saying here is that *it is in laying down one's life that joy comes to us.*

In this place He is using a trilogy of words. The first of the three is *joy* and the second is *love.* These two words are certainly compatible and it is not hard to think of them together. One would imagine that the third word in the trilogy would be *peace,* or *hope,* or *grace,* or *mercy,* or any of those other words we usually associate with happiness. But He is joining joy and love with *death.* He is saying that joy and love and laying down our lives are three ideas that just naturally belong together. They are not mutually exclusive—like somebody said about the words *military intelligence.* They are friends and they travel hand-in-hand.

I am beginning to understand this a little bit. At the company I had a very good secretary. One of the things about an efficient secretary is that she keeps posted in your calendar and hers all the dates and appointments that are important. Each year she would mark my new calendar book with the days I wanted to remember—like birthdays and anniversaries. A few days before the day, Karen would begin reminding me that I should buy a gift and a card. This was helpful to me for I am like the man described in a little poem in the *Reader's Digest:*

> Anniversaries and birthdays
> How they complicate my life.
> For I'm an absent-minded husband
> of a present-minded wife.

Sometimes, I was especially busy and each day she would remind me again, and I would tell her that I had not forgotten. But when the day came and she asked me if I had been shopping yet, I had to say no. She knew the appointments for the day and knew that I would be busy all day long with one person or meeting after another, straight through lunch. In fact, by the time I would finish, it would be past time to get home for dinner. So she would say, "Do you want me to buy the present?"

"Well, yeah," I would weakly reply.

Did you ever give your wife an anniversary present that your secretary had bought? Well, it wasn't much fun to give and I suspect it wasn't much fun to receive, either, because all of the giver that was involved were some dirty green pieces of paper. And no matter how many of them it took, it still did not represent as much as it should have, because it did not have the giver's time, his love, or his thoughts. It only took me once to see that. There isn't much joy in giving what somebody buys and wraps for you.

When Jesus says *"A man should lay down his life,"* I believe that what He is trying to get us to see is that this is where joy and love are found. Not just for the receiver—but for the giver as well. He is reminding us to release our gifts and graces and let them flow out of us and into others, knowing that as we do, joy and love will come flowing back to us.

You know the process. Last week, when you were running late for work, the traffic was worse than ever because it had rained a little. The line at the traffic signal seemed interminable. Resisting the urge to do something constructive like blowing your horn, you impatiently waited. And some little old lady, or worse still, some big old dude, was trying to get your eye to see if you would let him pull out of the doughnut shop parking lot in front of you. In a burst of released humanity, you looked at him and smiled and signaled that you would wait so he could pull out. His relieved and grateful look told you he was late for work also and his boss was even grumpier than yours, if that could be. The signal changed and, as the traffic slowly started, the driver pulled ahead of you and waved his thanks and smiled at you in the rear-view mirror. And you nodded in acknowledgment and your day was already better.

It was a different feeling than the one that comes to you when you pull up within an eighth of an inch of the car in front and, with the concentration of a waitress, manage to totally ignore some poor benighted doughnut-eater. Something comes to you in the simple giving up of twenty-five feet of pavement and nine seconds on the clock.

Isn't that part of what He means?

Over the years I have observed a change in the way we celebrate Christmas at our house. The process of opening the gifts is taking longer and longer. When the kids were small, it didn't take very long at all.

At the house where we spent so many Christmases together, we couldn't see the living room from the bottom of the steps. On Christmas morning the rule was that the kids had to wait on the third step until Peg and I gave the word. We made the coffee and arranged all the presents and things that Santa Claus had brought, although I was never one to give him much of the credit. If I bought it, I put my name on the card. And when we were ready—poised with the camera—we gave the word and it was as if some starting gun had sounded. In an instant or so, in an explosion of tissue paper, little boys were transformed into cowboys and dolls found new mothers. But the moments were soon over when someone ran outside to ride a new bike or kick a ball. It was unbelievable how quickly a time so long awaited and prepared for could be over.

It is taking longer now—and the reason seems to be that nobody wants to open what *he got.* He had rather see somebody else open what *he has given.*

In the summer, while we were on vacation, Peg and Leigh were shopping together. Leigh finished and came out on the sidewalk where I was sitting with some other temporary shopping widowers. Peg bought something for Leigh and hid it away in her suitcase and kept it all fall. Once or twice, she thought she couldn't wait any longer to give it to Leigh, but she managed. And she had wrapped it and put it under the Christmas tree.

Now she is handing it to Leigh and kneeling in front of her, waiting for it to be opened. Leigh is like her mother, for which I am glad. All ribbons, paper, and boxes must be saved. First, she reads the card and then slowly and carefully she unwraps the gift. To Peggy, it seems like forever. But the moment finally comes and Leigh exclaims, "Oh—I saw that last summer—and I wanted it—but I just hated to ask!"

"I saw you see that last summer," Peg smiles, "and I thought it was so much like you, I bought it for you."

And Jesus is trying to explain to us who was the happiest person that morning.

Joy and *love* and *death* are the words He is using and He gathers them up with *should. Should* because this is how joy makes its way to you.

A second thing that is occurring to me in this phrase is that it is *in the process of laying down one's life that God's strength restores us.*

Last year I enjoyed the privilege of helping to fill the chaplaincy of my alma mater, Trevecca Nazarene College, here in Nashville. Actually, the pastor on the college church, good friend Ed Nash, was doing most of the work. To try to maintain some continuity in the spiritual life of the students, he and I had a chapel service each week. He was nice to insist that I do the speaking. Naturally, when someone is willing to do all the work and let me do all the talking, it's a job in which I'm interested.

For the fall quarter I was using the first chapter of Ephesians as a background for my talks. Most of my previous speaking from Ephesians had been in the third chapter, so I was seeing some new things. One of these thoughts was a different way of perceiving the relationship of God's strength and our weakness. But the new and almost startling insight that came to me here was the idea that our weakness also determines the manner and the measure in which God's strength comes to us.

In this chapter Paul writes of the collective wealth that is ours in Christ. It included:

"every spiritual blessing"
"being chosen"
"acceptance"
"release"
"forgiveness"
"wisdom and insight"
"knowledge of His purpose"
"unity"

All these things are our heritage in Christ and Paul calls them "our share."

He goes on to write:

"you have heard the message"
"believed it"
"become incorporate in Christ"
"and received the Holy Spirit"

These folks had had all their crisis experiences, too. But still he prays that God would give them "spiritual powers of vision," that their eyes may be opened" so that they would "*know* . . . the wealth and glory of the share" and that they might *see* "how vast are the resources of His power open to us who trust in Him."

But it is not easy to describe the power of God. You don't know to what to compare it. There aren't enough words and you can't use a yardstick. How do you say what He is and what He can be to us? Paul says that His power is "*measured* by the strength and might which He exerted in Christ when he raised Him from the dead. . . ."

Sometimes I think we have a notion that Christ was kind of *pretending* in the tomb. He was dead, in a sense maybe, but somehow He was really just waiting until Easter morning when He would get up and come on out. But it was not like that at all. He was *dead-dead.*

The silence of death was interrupted only by the muffled sobbing of the women who stayed and the occasional steps of the guards as they moved about to keep themselves awake.

He had said He was *life*—but He was dead.

He had said He was the *way*—but He took the same old road that man had always traveled.

He had said He was *living water*—but there was only a puddle left in the memory of a few men and it was soon going to evaporate in the noonday sun.

He had said He was *bread*—but there were barely enough crumbs left to show what had been on the plate.

He had said He was the *light of the world*—but His tomb was as dark as every man's.

He was *dead.*

To paraphrase a sentence of Flannery O'Connor's, "You can't be any 'weaker' than dead."

And so God, the Father, who had breathed the breath of life into man, leans low and once again blows life into His Son. It throbs through His body. Decay and death are stopped. He shakes away the burial clothes. Jesus was raised from the dead—*but it was because He had been willing to die.*

If Jesus had rather not gotten involved; if He had managed to stay aloof from the events of that momentous week in Jerusalem; if the crowds and the noise had only given Him a headache and a mild rash, then a headache and a mild rash would have become the boundaries to His Father's ability to help Him. The measure of the vulnerability and weakness of Jesus became the boundaries of God's power to help. Death—and only death—brings resurrection and life.

And I think Jesus is trying to tell us that the Father wants to do more for us than we can ever believe. But it is in our deaths, our defeats, our emptinesses, our discouragements, our vulnerabilities, our weaknesses, our surrenders, that He can help us. For He can only *pick up* what we are willing to *lay down.*

No wonder Jesus says *should.*

Since I am a preacher and a would-be teacher, you will have to forgive me for a moment of review. I want to tell you again the two things I have told you, before I tell you one more.

We *should lay down our lives* because that is the way we are made joyful. *It is the way joy comes to us.* And we *should* because that is the way we are made strong. *It is the way His help comes to us.* And then, we should lay down our lives because that is the way they become redemptive. *It is the way love flows out of us.*

We used to sing a song called, "Ten Thousand Angels." It was popular in its day and rather widely used. The thing that it says best is that, although Christ could have called *ten thousand angels* to His rescue, He suffered and died alone.

A friend of mine on the West Coast, Fred Bock, has

an offbeat sort of humor. Once he was telling us about some songs that he had written that just missed popularity by one word. If he had just changed one word the song would have been widely used. One of his titles was "He Could Have Called Ten Thousand Locusts." If you knew Fred, that would be as funny to you as it is to me.

But I was thinking about that later. Jesus really could have called ten thousand of anything He wanted to call—angels, armies, legions, floods, even locusts. But we are not redeemed because He *could have*, we are redeemed because he *wouldn't*.

Dietrich Bonhoeffer wrote about the death of Christ. The following passage from *Letters and Papers From Prison* is even more meaningful because he wrote it when he was very close to his own death.

> God lets Himself be pushed out of the world on to a cross. He is weak and powerless in the world, and that is precisely the way, the only way, in which He is with us and helps us. . . . Christ helps us, not by virtue of his omnipotence, but by the virtue of His weakness and suffering. . . . Only the suffering God can help.

In his book, *The Crucified God,* Jürgen Moltmann writes about this same deeply moving truth.

> . . . the faith . . . derives its vitality not from Christ healing as a superhuman, divine miracle-worker, but on the contrary from the fact that He brings help through His wounds. . . . It can be summed up by saying that suffering is overcome by suffering, and wounds are healed by wounds. . . . Through His own abandonment by God, the crucified Christ brings God to those who are abandoned by God.

As always the truth comes to us two ways through Jesus. First, He tells us in words and phrases that we can understand. "Unless a grain of wheat is willing to fall into the ground and die it will live out its days alone." "A man should lay down his life." But He also shows us. The truth is *fleshed out* so we all can see it.

And Jesus' death on the cross was not some unfortunate act that lay in stark contrast to the way He lived. His living and His dying were lovely in their sameness. For He was always giving away parts and pieces of Himself. The choices that He made were choices that led Him to the cross. The conflicts came because He could not keep from *laying Himself down* when the misfits and the needy came to Him. If He could have walked on by the cripple beside the pool that morning, He would not have been accused of breaking the Sabbath and He would not have aroused the wrath of those who only knew the law. And they would not have plotted His death. But He couldn't and He didn't.

Isaac Watts wrote a phrase in what I guess is my favorite hymn, "When I Survey The Wondrous Cross." The phrase is *sorrow and love flow mingled down*. Jesus is telling us and showing us that *sorrow and love* go together. And that it is sorrow which gives love its redemptive quality.

We are not helped in our afflictions because He has the power to help. We are comforted and redeemed because His heart is broken. It is not the strength of His arm—it is the vulnerability of His heart that reaches out to us.

Let me tell you one more story about being in the hospital last spring. I had been in before but still I was impressed with the tremendous forward strides that have been made in the practice of medicine. Machines and equipment have been developed that greatly aid in the doctor's task of diagnosing the problems, prescribing the treatment, and alleviating suffering.

Some things, though, still have not changed. For

instance, you can get a private hospital room but you still can't get a private hospital *gown*.

I observed that medicine, or the art of healing, is practiced (not a very reassuring term) in concentric circles that seem to be at various distances from you.

For instance, the x-ray department seemed rather far removed from me. I could always tell when I was going to be taken down there because the nurse quietly removed my water container at midnight and they left me off the breakfast list the next morning. Finally they would come and roll me down in a wheelchair and I would join in waiting with a host of other people who also had not had any breakfast. We were in an assortment of robes that would have made the church drama director white with envy. It was cold down there. You could hang meat in the x-ray department. You would think with all the modern miracles the x-ray table could be preheated. But I guess that would violate some privilege of medical science. X-ray was always a department—never a he or a she to me.

The circle came closer to me when my doctor came. We are very fortunate to have a compassionate, caring person for our family doctor. He felt my pulse and listened to my heart and talked to me. He answered my questions and Peggy's and studied my chart and wrote the "orders" so that I would be as comfortable as possible while on the road to being well.

But the circle of medicine which seems to surround me most tightly was practiced in the wee hours of the morning when, for the fourth time within an hour, I pressed the call button and someone answered,

"Can I help you?"

"Yes, I need you again."

And someone came and cleaned me where I was dirty and touched me where I hurt. And she remade my bed and tucked the covers under my chin once more and said to me, "Now go back to sleep, but call me if you need me."

I mumbled some dumb apology for bothering her and making such a mess again. And the answer was, "That's okay. That's why we're here."

A lot of sharing of our lives is on some outer circle where it doesn't cost us much at all, but I am beginning to believe that the true, meaningful experience of our lives will be touching, and washing, and smiling, and lifting. And all along there will be less and less of us because of places and hours and people where we have left part of ourselves.

In the novel, *So Big,* Edna Ferber has one of her characters say, "You're too smooth. I like 'em bumpy."

I think Jesus is saying to us:

"You're going out to live life.
Don't take too good care of yourself,
find some things that count,
stick your neck out,
spill some blood,
spread some love.
The sin is not in breaking the rules—
it's in holding back."

We *should.*

Not a Field, But a Farm

And so it came to be decision time.

A few days after my forty-ninth birthday, I was up early and seated in my big, brown, tweed, swivel chair. My thoughts were about as scattered as the books and papers in front of me on the antique walnut table that served as my desk. It was a time for thinking and reflection on this last long holiday weekend before the summer ended. And I welcomed the peace and quiet of my study.

I was reading some words Rainer Maria Rilke, the German poet, had written in answer to a younger would-be poet's letters to him. He told him about the place from which the poetry of one's life must come.

> Therefore save yourself from these general themes and seek those which your own everyday life offers you; describe your sorrows and desires, passing thoughts and the belief in some sort of beauty—describe all these with loving, quiet, humble sincerity and use, to express yourself, the things in your environment, the images

from your dreams, and the objects of your memory. *If your daily life seems poor, do not blame it: blame yourself, tell yourself that you are not poet enough to call forth its riches;* for to the creator there is no poverty and no poor indifferent place. (Italics mine.)

Slowly I had been becoming more and more aware of the inner continuity of my life; of its movement and flow; and of the almost imperceptible signs of changes in direction. But changes and decisions do not come easily to me.

Nearly thirty-four years before, I had heard Him say, "Follow me." Even then the words were not written in the sky. But I had started out, as best I knew, to live in answer to their claim on me. They had taken me to college and to seminary and into the pastorate. There had been little groups of people in tiny churches in Tennessee and in Missouri while I was in school and then California and Florida when I had graduated. My inability to shepherd those churches into growth finally brought me to discouragement and resignation. Peg and I had two little boys by then, and we put all our stuff in a trailer and headed home to Nashville.

Twenty years had sped by. My dad had made a place for me in the family music business. In those early days there were only five of us in one office, but the business had grown and expanded far beyond everyone's fondest dreams and expectations. Meanwhile, Peg and I had built a house by the lake, and three more children had come into the family.

For a long time after we returned to Nashville, I thought the business was only temporary for me and that the call would come and we would again go to pastor. But the phone had not rung, and over the years other ways to follow Him had seemed to open up through the company and in the church where we had been reared.

The years had brought peace and prosperity to us. There had been some illness and darkness, too, which gave us some appreciation of the sunshine. They had also brought an accumulation of responsibilities and pressures that now seemed to fill my every waking hour with activity and concern.

So that morning in my study many things were reminding me of Leigh's words, *I just got myself back*. And I was thinking of all the things and tasks with which I was *going steady*. And out of all the past and the present, I seemed to be hearing a familiar voice saying words that I had heard before. They were calling for a *new commitment to an old invitation*. The words were *Follow me*.

Follow me—simple words but words with new and varied meanings as they come to us again and again across our days.

Peter, too, had heard them more than once. And every time they were spoken to him, they called him to places of deepened commitment. That first afternoon by the shore he was fishing with his brother, Andrew. He could not begin to imagine where he would be going or that he would never really be coming back. But the Man and His words, *Follow me*, were so compelling that with hardly a glance at each other, he and Andrew had pulled in the net and tied the boat to the shore and started out.

He understood them a little better, maybe, but still not fully when they came to him again over in Caesarea Philippi. At least he knew *who* he was following now. Some people might think Jesus was John the Baptist and some might think He was Elias or another prophet. But Peter was sure he knew—Jesus was the Christ. What he didn't know yet was what it was going to mean to follow this Christ, the Son of the living God. It was too soon to know what Jesus meant when He was saying, "Whoever will come after me, let him deny himself, and take up his cross, and *follow me.*"

Finally, though, Peter had come full circle—once again he was standing on the shoreline of all he knew and loved. It was morning, a morning after the resurrection and Jesus cooked breakfast for Peter and those with him. Now they are seated around the dying embers of the fire which Jesus Himself had built. And the question comes to Peter, not once, or twice, but three times, "Peter, do you love Me more than all of this?"

And three times Peter looked at all the things around him—all the things which were precious to him—all the things that made his life happy and worthwhile.

There was the boat. He had loved that boat since the first time his father had taken him out on it. His mother had argued, and lost, that he was too little to be going out on a boat. His father had said he could go and from that day on there was never a doubt in his mind what he was going to be—he was a fisherman.

There were the nets. He had hung them up to dry after a long day of fishing. He had mended them until he knew almost every knot in them. And he had cast them into the sea and hauled them in, jumping and splashing with fish.

There, in the morning sunlight, lay the village. He knew it, too, like the back of his hand. He had climbed every fence and walked on every wall when he was a boy. It was his home.

And now he looks again into the eyes of Jesus and gives his answer, "Lord, you know I do. You know everything, even my heart and You know that I love You—more than these."

And once again Jesus repeated to him two words. Two words—simple enough to be understood and obeyed in an instant; but two words so rich and deep that one may easily spend his whole life with them as his guide and never know all their significance. Two words—*follow Me.*

And these were the words that were coming to me on that end-of-a-summer morning. In a sense I, too, was standing on the shoreline of my life. About me, almost within my vision, was all I knew best and loved most. I picked up my pen and a pad and began to write—to myself—to my family—and to Him.

Labor Day
7:00 A.M.

I am trying very hard to *read my own mind.* . . . Am I honestly dedicating myself to a new purpose? Is it a deliberate *getting myself back,* to use Leigh's phrase, an honest deep-down desire to reduce life to some simpler form so that in these days I may be closer to the Source? Am I hoping, praying that this will give me greater usefulness, effectiveness, more time?

Or is it a natural tiredness and a corresponding desire to get rid of a set of problems, including a recognition of my own failures in judgment?

Am I choosing a new life or simply copping out on the present one?

Further, are the things that seem to be happening really signs—the log house, Mike's leaving the company to go to seminary, Robert's decision to strike out on his own, my college chaplaincy, speaking, the retreats—are these and many more things saying: Now is the time? And even the business itself—the pressures, the mistakes, the prospects, my very reluctance to push on—are those signs?

In some ways it is not necessarily so noble. I honestly believe we will be all right financially, probably far better off than most people. But even if we were not—I think I am ready for fewer things and simpler pleasures.

Even the process about the business—from thinking I would not want to sell; of my responsibilities to staff, people, artists, and to the family tradition—has changed. The questions about leaving the present position of the company or to give it my best for another three to five years, hoping to make it hum and then to sell my part and do the things I wish I had time for now.

But this seems to be a no-win proposition too—if I don't succeed, then I should not have stayed. And if I could succeed, it would only mean more time, more promises to more people, and more reasons not to be able to stop then.

The discussions with Robert helped. In many ways I share the deepest dreams of the company with him—and even if we could establish the things we both desire in the three to five years—would he be at the same point then as I am now? Wondering how many poems I could have written, or how many walks I missed with Peg, how many trips to see Mike and Gwen and Leigh that we could not take?

It seems to be the time to change. I only want to do the thing that will make *more of me*—not less. I believe I have come to a place in both ability and discipline to find and pursue avenues of service and fulfillment greater than those that come connected with my present position.

In terms of the children—I believe that Robert and Mike have good systems of values. Mike's direction is maybe more clearly defined just now. But Robert's is just as deep—if not deeper—through adversity. He is maybe more idealistic—but the stuff is there to give his life purpose and direction. And Leigh, she is a wonder to me—what she is and is becoming. I feel that fewer things—possessions of ours—might make it better for whomever she might choose as a husband. I don't mean her love of things—I mean the specter of competition or achievement it places on her husband consciously or unconsciously. The fate of sons-in-law in the Benson clan has been a tragedy. It is a tragedy we have not been able to avoid either, for in some respects the business—with its day-and-night demands for time, energy, thought—have also contributed to the grief of divorce that has engulfed our family.

Tom and Patrick are at important, crucial places in their lives. I believe strongly in them both. But I want to make a statement to them that my own head is on straight about values in life. There should be no discrepancy, or as little as possible, between what I say about true values in life and what I am willing to sacrifice to the pursuit and maintenance of them.

There is also the deep pain within that grows out of being a man who would go about and speak of the power and strength of love and feeling estrangement, hurt, frustration and, indeed, anger that has grown out of the complicated interworking of a family business.

Last and deepest of all the personal things, I think it is time to begin a new and deeper life with Peg. A life, I think, that is cultivated by walks on a beach, or through the woods, or reading, or listening to music together—a life that needs time. In the ongoing of our lives together, the moments when we have only been an eyelash apart have been the best. Speed, pace, pressure, schedules, all rob us of what can be between us.

Finally I guess the question of what God wants me to be and what I want to be for Him is calling insistently to me. There are the visions and hopes about my life that arise from time to time. . . . When Reuben was here and spoke at the church on "Getting Ready for God's Good Thing." . . . Or hearing the words of Glaphre which I can't even quote correctly—but which continue to burn just the same—about the need for new levels of devotion. . . . Tozer's words from *The Pursuit of God* about Abraham when he offered up Isaac, "a grand old man standing face-to-face with God." And there are the prayers of people in whom I really believe—and they seem to see me somewhere else doing other things.

All these things seem to beckon me onward to a new road. There are things that stand in my way—like admitting and feeling failure or, worse still, knowing or thinking that some of those I set out to compete with will say I failed. And there are the perks of being president. It is rewarding in so many ways. And the people I have attracted and to whom, in one way or another I have made commitments. The management team as well as the people—the Jeanne Pikes, Mary Davises, Glenn Smothermans, Matt Steinhauers—and all the others. There are the things I started that caused other people to make decisions. It is not easy to feel that I am going back on promises I made to them.

Still and all—I believe I must turn a corner. This day I am going to write the letter that starts the process of problem-solving—extricating, admitting defeat, winning, losing, or whatever is involved.

I pray that it will be in an honest desire to let the deepest messages of my life be that I live my life with an "open hand."

For I hear the words of Jesus:
"What does all that matter to you?
Follow Me."

I do not want to try to overdramatize this decision. I know that resigning from a company is a long way from nailing theses on the door at Wittenburg. But it was a turning point for me. It was an acknowledgment, an affirmation that more than anything else I wanted to be *in quest of the shared life*.

I wish now that I had written this book that afternoon. What I was *going to do* is probably more impressive than what *I've done*. But it was to be a fresh start for me. And I believe that at least part of the great beauty hidden in the words, *follow me,* is the insight that every day, every hour, and every moment provides a chance to begin again. And most of us have a deep need to find the way and the place to start over.

In the intervening months I have found that I have followed the pathway with broken and uneven steps. There have been warm, happy days like Christmas and there have been *unvolunteered for* weeks in the hospital. There have been mornings in the study when ideas and insights came to me *in my own words* and I was so moved by them I could hardly scribble them down. And I have also written down words that were so dull and dry and devoid of ideas that they seemed to blow off the page before I could get to the end of the sentence. There have been the beginnings of a new richness in our family relationships that the simpler, slower pace has brought although even before the reading of the "Labor Day Paper" my family surrounded me with love and support. Still, at times, my quest has come so close to selfishness that Peg kindly but aptly remarked: "It is hard to live with a saint." And the earnestness in her voice, lightly disguised with humor, made me know she was not talking to one.

Life has come along with its usual mixture of the good and the bad and the monotonous. As usual, I am not sure that I even knew which was which at the time. But I have reaffirmed some things that I have known for a long time but tend to forget.

One of those is that the quest is just what the word implies. It is always a quest. The shared life is not a destination; it is a journey. It is not an arrival; it is a departure. It is as Robert Raines says in *To Kiss The Joy*, "The continuity of our throbbing life is not permanence, but newness . . ."

Matthew tells us a story that seems to me to be saying this same thing. Mary Magdalene went out to the tomb of Jesus early in the morning on the first day of the week. And an angel said to her, "This is the place where they laid Him, but He is not here. He has *gone before you* into Galilee and you will see Him there." The quest is not a shrine, it is a pilgrimage and always He goes before us. Even the empty tomb is not a stopping place—indeed it is but a milestone on the way.

Jesus Himself tells us about those who were hungry and thirsty. They are the ones who will be filled. It is a paradox but it is true. Because we are hungry, we are filled and because we are filled, we are hungry. It is as Julian writes, "I had Him and I lacked Him, I found Him and I sought Him."

One of the things that I love about my church is that she is always challenging me. She never lets me think that I have arrived. When I was younger I sometimes took issue with some of her pronouncements, especially when they seemed to invade those parts of my life which I felt were outside her prerogatives. But she has steadfastly maintained that nothing is neutral in the quest. And her insistent teachings were always that the more one becomes, the more he sees his need of becoming. The deeper the roots of one's life go, the more he is impressed with their shallowness. The more conscious one is of closeness to God, the more he is aware of the distance that separates him from God. And we realize that we are not fields—we are farms.

This began to come to me in the parable of the sower. Jesus loved to tell us about the Father, about His will and purpose and about His love and compassion for us. He tried to tell us what the Father and the kingdom were really *like*. He seems to know that we *like* things that are *like*. So again and again He tells us they are: like a man who . . . , like a mustard seed, like yeast, like ten virgins, like a king. When we listen to Him, we can always find a peg on which to hang the truth He comes to share.

One afternoon He was standing on the prow of a boat that had been tied to the shore. He was telling the people who had gathered at the water's edge about the Father. Over in the distance, perhaps, they could all see a field and, in it, a man sowing seed. But even if there hadn't been a sower in the afternoon sunlight, they could picture him slowly going back and forth across the field, scattering the seed with the motion of his arm and digging into the bag slung beneath his arm for another handful.

And Jesus continued with *His* planting:

> A sower went out to sow his seed,
> And as he sowed some of the seed fell on the path,
> where it was trampled on and where
> the birds could come and eat it.
> Some of the seed fell on rock and when
> it came up it withered and died
> for it had no moisture.
> Some of the seed fell in among thistles
> and the thistles grew up with it
> and choked it.
> Some of the seed fell into good soil and grew
> and yielded a hundredfold.

This simple story must have been readily understood by all of those who were listening to Him that day. I know that I have always understood its rather transparent truth and knew just who He was talking about, haven't you?

Well, I didn't know just exactly who He meant by *path* and *rock* and *thistles,* but at least I knew who He was talking about when He spoke of good, rich, deep soil that produced as much as a hundredfold. It is very obvious, to me at least, that He was talking about me. Or was He?

Lately I have been thinking that this is a story about a foursome that consists of me—and me and me and me. I'm old *Mr. Goodsoil* himself, of course, but I also answer to *Pathway, Rocky,* or *Thistles.* The parable is all about me. And it is coming to me that I am not a field—I am a farm.

I have some fields that I have cultivated with His help and they have and do bring forth an increase. But across some of the land there are pathways that have been trampled and hardened because I always went the easiest and shortest way. I took them over and over. And the commerce of life has gradually worn them down.

Again, it is not hard for me to remember my dreams and plans at the beginning of many a planting season. I have watched with excitement and enthusiasm, tender young shoots springing up out of the ground. But I also recall the tears and frustration that were mine as they wilted and died because there was no depth to my preparation and commitment.

Down across the creek from the field behind the barn, there is a patch of rich ground. It is already plowed and planted. But I suppose it is also filled with the seeds and roots of thorns and thistles and weeds that I have either invited to come or allowed to stay. And in time they will choke out the life that He wants to bring me in increase. I am not a field—I am a farm.

Let me show you a new way to read this story. I hear it like this:

A sower goes out to sow—
some seed falls on the path
some falls on rocks
some falls among thorns
and some into good soil
and the sower goes out to sow.
Some seed falls on the path
some falls on rocks
some falls among thorns
and some into good soil
and the sower goes out to sow.
Some seed falls on the path
some falls on the rocks
some falls among thorns
and some into good soil.
and the sower goes out to sow.

You should read it about ten times this way until you begin to realize that always the *Sower goes out to sow*. Always He comes to you, never tiring, never discouraged that you have far more poor soil than you do good. Always He comes, never despairing of seeds that perish.

The late Thomas Merton in his book, *New Seeds of Contemplation*, writes about the myriad ways He comes to us:

> Every moment and every event of every man's life on earth plants something in his soul. For just as the wind carries thousands of winged seeds, so each moment begins with its germs of spiritual vitality that rest imperceptibly in the minds and hearts of men. Most of these unnumbered seeds perish and are lost, because men are not prepared to receive them: for such seeds as these cannot spring up anywhere except in the good soil of freedom, spontaneity and love.

And that morning in my study I seemed to be hearing Him say to me:

I'll plant the seeds;
You till the soil
I'll send the rain;
You chop the weeds.
I'll make the sunshine;
You scythe and gather.
I'll go before you;
You follow me.

He was quietly saying to me that I had gained all the insight that my present commitment could bring me. I had seen everything that there was to be seen in this place. He had taught me all He could teach me with what I had entrusted to Him. If I wanted to know what was on the far side of the horizon, I would have to follow on. Perhaps it would be harder now than it had been when I had started out as a sixteen-year-old—but still—I had to go.

And so I took the letter and I placed it on the desk of the chairman of the board. And I started out again to try to learn some of the newness and joy in those two simple words of invitation that He continues to extend to me.

The very next weekend I was headed west to speak to a group in retreat in the mountains of New Mexico. It was one of those marvelous weekends that only belong to September. The weather was perfect as I left home. It had rained off and on for the past few days and then very heavily the night before as Hurricane David had spent the last of its strength in a final assault on the western half of Tennessee. And now the world looked as if God had just washed it and hung it out to dry in the morning sunlight.

But the farther west we flew, the more cloudy it became. I changed planes in Dallas. If heaven is west of Nashville, I'm sure there'll be a layover in the Dallas-Fort Worth airport. As we drove across the desert the distant mountains were almost hidden in fog. At last we climbed the mountains in dense clouds and rain. When we finally arrived at the retreat grounds, it was cold and rainy. I wouldn't have been at all surprised to find a snowstorm. And I couldn't help thinking a little bit about how nice it would have been at home going to the football game with the boys.

It was almost suppertime when we got there and the evening service followed almost immediately. There was not very much time to get my mind and heart prepared. I spent what time there was in quietness among cases of canned goods and sacks of flour in the storage room just behind the kitchen.

The lodge itself was warm and friendly and so were the people. They pulled their chairs up close to the makeshift platform alongside the fire in the huge mountain stone fireplace. It was a good room in which to sing, and the songs and hymns rang through the lodge and began to bring us together as if huddled for warmth against the chill rain outside. There were the usual announcements and rules and greetings and then a time of prayer, and I was introduced.

With my battered NEB Version of the New Testament in my hand, I moved the few steps forward to the stand thinking to myself as I went:

Well, here you are, Mr. Speaker, you feel that you have some deep and lasting contribution to make to people like these who sit before you now. Here you are, let's hear it.

With a little humor and about the same amount of laughter in response, I began to reach out and probe for ways to establish a bond with the people gathered before me. With our heads bowed we sang another song or two and I prayed that somehow in these times we would be bound together in ways that would be helpful and life-changing to us all.

The Book opened easily to the fifteenth chapter of John and I began to read words and phrases that were so familiar to me now.

"I am the real Vine, and my Father is the Gardener."

"I am the Vine and you are the branches."

"He who dwells in me, as I dwell in Him, bears much fruit."

"Apart from Me . . . nothing . . . in Me . . . and My words . . . in you . . . you shall have it."

"A man should lay down his life for his friends."

"You are My friends."

"You did not choose Me: I chose you."

This was my Scripture place and my thoughts were centered around it.

Now you have to understand that I do not really have a fixed set of sermons or talks. Even though I may be speaking from the same verses over a long period of time, they are never the same talks. It is a process of growing and gathering and sifting. Some of the stories and points are the same, but they must find their shape in a given moment and at a given place for the people then and there.

Always I realize there are some people out there to whom I am speaking who have come with broken hearts and some who have come because their load was almost more than they can bear. And what I say to them must be *to them.* It cannot be something I am saying simply because I have said it before with some modicum of success. It is *to them* I want to speak.

And so I must try to have what I have gathered resting easily on my heart and mind so that I will be free to receive new thoughts about what I am to say and how I am to say it. When my spirit is really prepared and my heart is at peace, standing before people becomes both a *speaking and a hearing experience for me.* At times like these it seems that the Spirit is *drawing out of me* my experiences, thoughts, and hopes—and *adding to me* His revelation and newness. And I feel that I am both the host and a beggar at the door. And it is these moments of inspiration—both memory and manna—that lead me out to speak and to hear.

Unfortunately for me, and even more so for the audience, this doesn't always happen. And when I am speaking and not much comes to me—*not much comes to me.* And I must make my way along with some stories and jokes that I have jotted down on a card and stuck a page or two over from the place from which I had hoped to be delivering a message. And at such times the card looks dustier than death and I feel like I am serving leftovers to hungry, honored guests.

It is at times like these that I wish God would give me some kind of a sign that proved to everyone that indeed He had sent me. So when I was having trouble speaking I could at least show them the sign. But I do not seem to be equipped with a sign. One just goes in the *strength of knowing*. Or maybe if I had had some tremendous experience in the war but I was in the Boy Scouts during the great one, WW II. I wouldn't even mind having some fiery, pungent truth that I could zap everybody with.

By my only sign is *knowing*. The things I have to say are just simple, ordinary things that have been said before and better, as well. They do not have much meaning to others except for the quality which reveals the manner in which they came to me. I cannot always remember whether some of them are things that I have said to Him or whether they are things that He has spoken to me. I only know that they are things that we have talked about together as I have followed Him.

And people *know* when you *know*.

We are all prone to go forth in the supposed strengths of our name, our honors, our degrees, or whatever bits of reputation may have preceded us. But these trappings do not have any power to corroborate or authenticate the things of God. And they will not, indeed they *cannot*, become our credibility.

There used to be a particular name for the table on which they placed the elements of the Lord's Supper. They called it the *credence table* because it held the symbols of our Lord's blood and body. On it rested the things which give us validity in claiming to be the sons of God. And it is only the life of Christ through the spirit in us that can put our lives on the *credence table*.

And I am learning that the only thing that is really going to make a difference in the things I say and write comes when there is no discrepancy, no gap, no ground of misunderstanding between what my words and the Spirit of Life are saying. When *over* and *above* and sometimes *instead* of what I am actually saying, the Spirit says, *Yea verily, Amen, It's true,* my life and my speaking begin to say something. When His Spirit bears witness with my spirit, the quality of my *saying* is bound by the quality of my *following*.

My dedication certificate shows that my parents dedicated me back to the Lord when I was an infant in their arms. My baptism record shows that as a teenager I was baptized in the name of the Father and the Son and the Holy Ghost as an outward symbol of the work that was done within me. I have a letter of membership which shows I am a member of the same local church that my grandparents helped to found. Over my desk on my study wall hangs an ordination certificate which indicates that I am an elder in the Church of the Nazarene with all of the rights and privileges thereto. But only the imprint of His cross on my life and my undertaking show that I am His follower.

And during that weekend in the cold rain in New Mexico, the times of meeting were warm and free. The Word moved me. It spoke to me and in me and through me. *I knew and they knew that I knew.* And I was reminded: Wherever He would take you is worth the going.

I used to laugh with a friend of mine about what we were going to be when we grew up. It seemed like a funny thing to say in college, but it probably became less and less amusing as the years rolled by. My answer for a long time was that I wanted to decide by the time I was fifty years old and then I wanted to be it for five years and then promptly retire. It is becoming apparent to me that I really do not know what I am going to be when I grow up. I cannot tell you what all I believe He wants me to be or where all I think He is going to lead me. I can only pray that I will have the faith and courage to say whatever, wherever.

I hope I will be like the middle-ager who hit a double while playing baseball with his kids. He was on second. His breath was on first. But his heart was roaring around third toward home.

I know that *wherever* is a reckless word. There are no halfway houses on the road to *wherever.* I have to use it guardedly. Even now I have not gone far enough for it to be a word that is really mine. But I would like to learn to live and believe so that *wherever* will hold no fears for me. For one reason or another I am not always a follower. Sometimes I am afraid to go. Sometimes my life is so good that I do not want to leave where I am. But when I have gone and when I have allowed it to become my word, I want to say to you unreservedly, *wherever is worth going.* At times I have remained behind only to find myself surrounded with nothing. But sometimes I have also left all to go with Him and I have known His everything. And I am convinced if I would always go I would always be glad.

The quest—
  Wherever it takes you—go;
Whichever the task—do it;
  Wherever the burden—accept it;
Whenever it calls—answer it;
  Whichever the lesson—learn it;
However dark the path—follow Him,
  Because *wherever He takes you,*
    It is worth it.